Electric Language

Understanding the Message

Eric McLuhan

A BUZZ BOOK
FOR ST. MARTIN'S PRESS

ISBN 0-312-19088-3

Published by arrangement with
Stoddart Publishing Co. Limited, Toronto

First published in the United States by St. Martin's Buzz

First St. Martin's Buzz Edition July 1998

10 9 8 7 6 5 4 3 2 1
Text and cover design: Eskind Waddell

The biologists...speak of "outbreeding" and "inbreeding." As Mayr puts it, "most animals are essentially outbreeders, most microorganisms inbreeders."

With electricity, all this has changed totally. At present the entire mammalian world has become the microorganismic. It is the total individual cultures of the world, linguistically and politically, that have become the mammals, according to the old classifications of evolutionary hypothesis. It is the cultural habitat in which we have long been accustomed to think that people were contained that has now become the mammal itself, now contained in a new macrocosm or "connubium" of a super-terrestrial kind. Our technologies, or self-amputations, and the environments or habitats which they create must now become that matrix of that macrocosmic connubial bliss derided by the evolutionist. – Conclusion to *War and Peace in the Global Village: An inventory of some of the current spastic situations that could be eliminated by more feedforward.* By Marshall McLuhan and Quentin Fiore (New York: Bantam Books, 1968)

contents

Contents

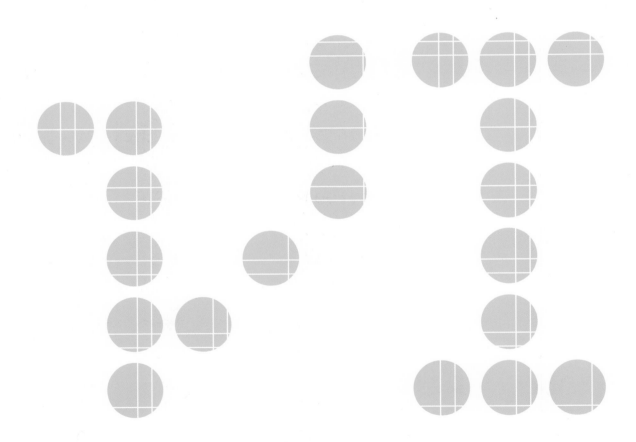

Introduction

Language is the greatest single gift and achievement of the human organism. Every language is an organ of perception, not simply a means of conveying ideas. The first mass medium, language confers order on both speaker and hearer. It provides identity. As an instrument of thought and imagination, it serves to penetrate and know both Nature and knower alike. Words put us in echoland: our words are things and the things we do and make are words. They echo us; they are us. They bear the pattern and music of our organs of perception and simultaneously work as means of awareness outside the body private and corporate, individual and social.

When we look at any situation through another situation we are using metaphor. And all language arises by this intensely intellectual process. Human languages themselves are the greatest of all works of art beside which the works of Homer, Virgil, Dante, and Shakespeare are minor variations. English – or any other – language is itself a massive organization of traditional experience that gives a detailed view of the world. Today, our increasing knowledge of the languages of primitive cultures has made it easy to see how language itself is the principal channel and view-maker of experience for people everywhere.

It is impossible for there ever to be a scientific concept that is not already implicit in the vernacular tongue of the scientist, and that has not been embedded there for many centuries. You cannot conceive a form of scientific hypothesis which is not already part of your own language, already implicit in that language. All the mathematics in the world are externalizations of certain linguistic patterns. What the poets have been saying for the last couple of centuries – now more widely appreciated – is that language

The Language of Media

itself encodes the greatest body of scientific intuition possible. The proportionalities in things, and between things and our senses, and embodied in language itself, are inexhaustible.

Any new technology releases some of that inexhaustible store of analogical intuition and experience which IS language. So radio, or computer, or internet, releases from within each user's language a whole body of resources which has been bound up there for centuries. This sudden burst of energy and awareness does not depend on concepts. It has to do with sensibility and observation – analogical perception, embedded right in the structure of language itself.

The simultaneous relations and new harmonies set up in this manner are utterly irrational and illogical; they appear to the rational-minded to be the return of chaos. But melody and sequence are just one way to order understanding; harmony and counterpoint open doors to dozens of other ways. Even chaos, we now find, conceals a world of infinite subtlety and patterns exquisite.

So why is it impossible to take one thing at a time in the world we live in? The global village is not a place where one thing happens at a time. Everything happens there at once (multitasking). What we must have in order to survive, therefore, is a means of coping with an all-at-once world. The artist and philosopher can perhaps help here. Harmony can be made of a great mass of seemingly disconnected fragments, but it is impossible to have visual order made of a vast unassorted mass of data, such as typifies every moment of existence in the electronic age. You cannot fill it all in. At electric speed, everything happens at once: there is no sequence, and everything that happens influences everything else, at the same time.

With monotonous repetition we hear on every hand: "This isn't an innovation, it's a revolution." "We live in an age of transition." "Things will be different after this." Whether uttered by responsible people or by morons these remarks, and countless others like them, have no meaning. They are spoken in a trance of inattention while the reason is in permanent abeyance. They are typical of people who no longer understand the world they have made and in which, as robots, they function day by day.

The essays below all make certain assumptions. They take for granted that human technologies are, literally, human utterances – outerings or extensions of the organism that uses them.

Mallarmé wrote his most difficult poem, "Un Coup de Dés," in newspaper format. He saw, as did James Joyce a century later, that the basic forms of communication – whether speech, writing, print, press, telegraph, or photography – necessarily were fashioned in close accord with human cognitive activity. The more extensive the mass medium, the closer it must approximate to our cognitive faculties. It cannot be otherwise: were we to contrive an extension of the senses of an amoeba or of some vegetation or some insect or a frog, the result might be of clinical interest but that only. It would be of no practical service to human communication.

Animals evolve by incorporating into their bodies the new technology, whether by growing longer teeth or by modifying their digestive systems. Human evolution works in the opposite manner. With the first inventions, human evolution suddenly shifted from the realm of biology to that of technology. Animals incorporated; we discorporated. We extended into the environment various parts of the body, various limbs and organs and, with electricity, the central nervous system. Most recently, computer technology and its children now extend around the globe the hemispheres and other elements and organs of the brain. It remains only to extend the mind itself.

The crowd in electric form is not a new kind of association but a new form of being, one in which we all participate, like it or not. Radio put us in the Global Village. Contrary to popular supposition, the Global Village is no ideal haven but a congested place which exaggerates the most ancient antipathies and differences and in which privacy is impossible. Television ushered in the Global Theater, in which everyone is "in role" at all times. The Global Theater admits no spectators, only actors, just as Spaceship Earth allows for no passengers, only crew. We have no choice in the matter. The computers and various networks that link us bring about a new condition of massive loss of identity by means of enhanced participation in depth in electronic processes. As information levels rise, "subjects" disappear and the differences between things melt away. As participation levels rise, human identities also dissolve. In turn, this loss generates a thirst for roots and a primal hunger for belonging – to groups.

Consequently, separatism of every sort replaces nationalism and all other kinds of rational allegiance instituted during the last couple of centuries. Our electric time demands a radically different feel for causation and causality. Rational, sequential causality provides no means whatever of coming to grips with the transforming power of electric media. Cause-and-effect has lost its grip except on the most superficial level of everyday affairs, in much the same way that Newton's three laws of motion have given way to Einsteinian relativity in contemporary affairs. Today, most of the effects of any innovation occur before the actual innovation itself. In a word, a vortex of effects tends, in time, to become the innovation. It is because human affairs have been pushed into pure process by electronic technology that effects can precede causes and software and information replace hardware artifacts. *Ground* always precedes *figure* and it is to an analysis of *ground*-effects that media study has to turn to remain relevant.

The ordinary sociological and futurological approaches are helpless in the face of these forces because they follow content-bound, linear tracks. They provide no room for reversal, or novelty, and assume a rational, consistent way of seeing. But projections of the present in terms of trends, etc., concentrate on *figure* and ignore *ground*, that is, media. The study of *ground* has traditionally been available only in the arts and as result not of theory but of training of perception and sensibility.

These considerations are of profound significance for our cultural institutions, as the *ground* of the West orientalizes electrically and the *ground* of the East west-ernizes. Electric experience holds few novelties for the Easterner, but it brings him into direct participation with Westernized experience for the first time. The first, second, and third worlds so dear to the press and politicians have now been displaced by a fourth world of electric information and imagery carried by satellite and the internets – a world in which we are all equally primitive. On the nets, everything is decentralized, even being. Everybody is a nomad, in the mode of hunter on a frontier, which also means the end of individualism and the rise of "characters" or roles.

Power, too, decentralizes while established bureaucracies of every kind melt away and dissolve. This means of course a shift to a completely new form of culture and with it a new and vital role for the arts, not, as formerly, as a specialist activity but as basic survival training; not as the ivory tower but as the control tower. The arts provide the indispensable means of training navigators in the new environ-ments precisely because they set aside concepts and focus on tuning ground and attuning sensibility.

Arachne or Penelope: Queen of the Net, Mistress of the Web?

Homer, Hesiod, and the preliterate poets encoded in their verses the full encyclopedia of their arts and sciences. By the word recited and sung, a hypnotic and mimetic spell bound culture and society. Memories were strong and vigorous. Precisely the same conditions apply today among the young with their songs and costumes, minus the encyclopedic knowledge.

But comes the written, alphabetic word: memory decays. The goddess Athena takes over as governess of social and intellectual affairs, and also her city, Athens, where the civilized gather and prosper. Outside the gates live the *barbaroi*, those who lack articulate speech and can only howl *"bar-bar-bar."* Athena was patroness of sweet reason; under her tutelage, Western civilization grew amid rhetoric and writing. The great epic poets give place to the theatrical poets and lyrical poets with their private voices. Abstract philosophical thought was the latest technology.

Although Athena's sway has held for twenty-four centuries, the electric age demands a new image. Rational detachment and abstraction have lost their appeal and their cogency. No longer is the city – or any mere place – "where the action is." In the age of the Internet, the center is no-where and now-here, everywhere at once. Everywhere is both center and periphery, placeless and boundless. We live "in the broadest way immarginable." What kind of patroness would suit this virtual world of the net and the web?

Many today have decided on the ancient web-crawler, Arachne, the maiden renowned for her skill at spinning and weaving. Ovid gives this account of her:

Neither for place of birth nor birth itself had [Arachne] fame, but only for her skill. Her father, Idmon of Colophon, used to dye the absorbent wool for her with Phocaean purple. Her mother was now dead; but she was low-born herself, and had a husband of the same degree. Nevertheless the girl, Arachne, had gained fame for her skill throughout the Lydian towns, although she herself had sprung from a humble home and dwelt in the hamlet of Hypaepa. Often, to watch her wondrous skill, the nymphs would leave their own vineyards on Timolus' slopes, and the water-nymphs of Pactolus would leave their waters. And 'twas the pleasure not alone to see her finished work, but to watch her as she worked; so graceful and deft was she. Whether she was winding the rough yarn into a new ball, or shaping the stuff with her fingers, reaching back to the distaff for more wool, fleecy as a cloud, to draw into long soft threads, or giving a twist with practised thumb to the graceful spindle, or embroidering with her needle: you could know that Pallas [Athena] had taught her. Yet, she denied it, and, offended at the suggestion of a teacher ever so great, she said, "Let her but strive with me; and if I lose there is nothing which I would not forfeit." – Ovid, *Metamorphoses* (Trans. Frank Justus Miller, Loeb Classical Library. Cambridge, Mass.: Harvard University Press, 1916. Rpt., 1971), VI, 7-25

Athena herself hears of the challenge, and takes it up. They hold a competition. Athena weaves an image of the gods in their glory. Arachne, imprudently, weaves one of mortals being gulled by the gods: Europa, Asterie, Leda, and many others. And she had the bad taste (and worse judgment) to beat Athena:

Not Pallas nor Envy himself, could find a flaw in [Arachne's] work. The golden-haired goddess [Athena] was indignant at her success, and rent the embroidered web with its heavenly crimes; and as she held a shuttle of Cytorian boxwood, thrice and again she struck Idmonian Arachne's head. The wretched girl could not endure it, and put a noose about her bold neck.

As she hung, Pallas lifted her in pity, and said: "live on, indeed, wicked girl, but hang thou still; and let this same doom of punishment (that thou mayest fear for future times as well) be declared upon thy race, even to remote posterity." So saying, as she turned to go she sprinkled her with the juices of Hecate's herb; and forthwith her hair, touched by the poison, fell off, and with it both nose and ears, and the head shrank up; the whole body also was small; the slender fingers clung to her side as legs; the rest was belly. Still, from this she ever spins a thread; and now, as a spider, she exercises her old-time weaver-art. – *Metamorphoses, VI, 129-145*

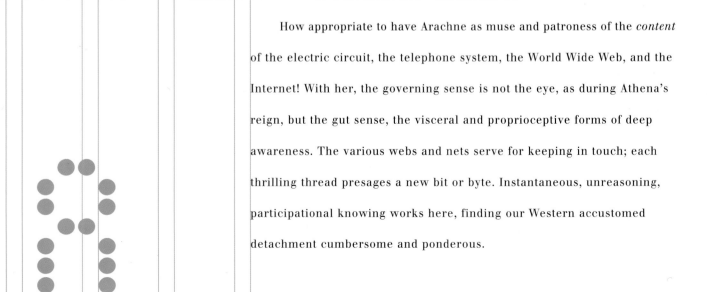

How appropriate to have Arachne as muse and patroness of the *content* of the electric circuit, the telephone system, the World Wide Web, and the Internet! With her, the governing sense is not the eye, as during Athena's reign, but the gut sense, the visceral and proprioceptive forms of deep awareness. The various webs and nets serve for keeping in touch; each thrilling thread presages a new bit or byte. Instantaneous, unreasoning, participational knowing works here, finding our Western accustomed detachment cumbersome and ponderous.

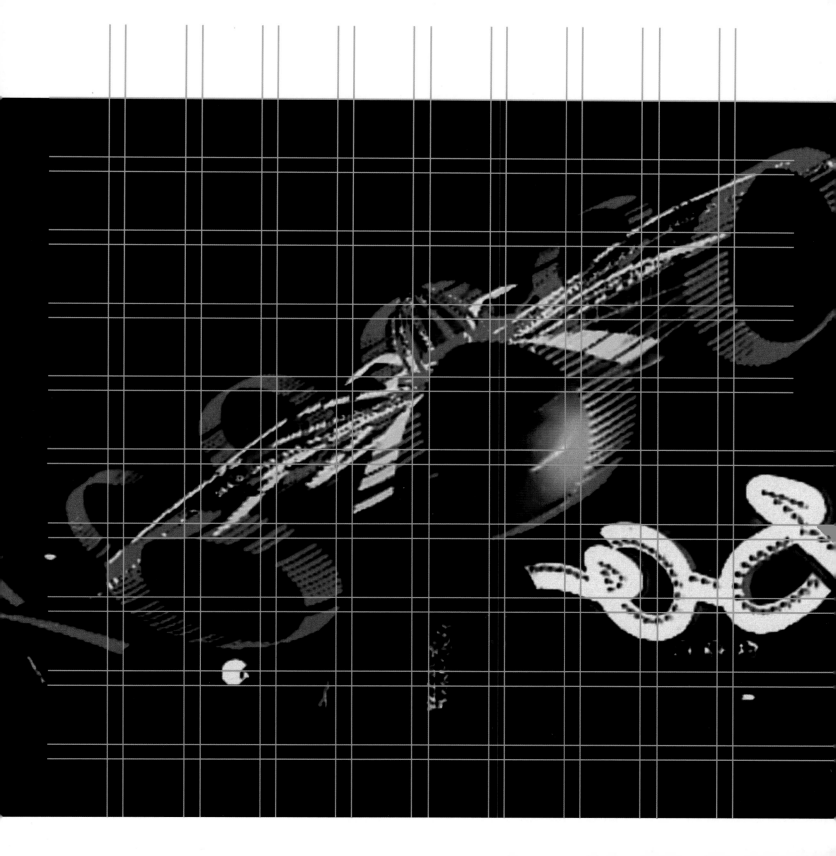

Yet, while there is a great deal to be said for assigning this matriarch as guiding spirit of the *content* of the net and the web, I think there is another, even better suited to the task of patroness of the circuit and the net.

Electricity is a monarchical form, not democratic: for patroness it requires not a commoner but a queen. Besides, Arachne, after all, made something from her spinning and weaving. She transformed matter, in a way, and was in turn herself transformed because of her impudence and imprudence.

But the World Wide Web is not in the process of becoming some other thing; the Internet is not about to finally realize its real nature as a product, a thing apart. Both the WWW and the Internet ARE. They exist. If they change, they change in size only, by growing and shrinking, for they already have attained their essential natures. They need, then, a deity that combines concern for weaving and so on with an emphasis on being rather than on becoming.

Homer gives us one such: the wife of King Odysseus, Queen Penelope.

Penelope personifies constancy and circumspection: often Homer bestows upon her the epithet "circumspect Penelope." She emphasizes duration, that is, being, transformation without direction or goal. Several times Homer describes her stratagem, always with the same words. Here, for example, one of the suitors narrates:

She set up a great loom in her palace, and set to weaving a web of threads long and fine. Then she said to us: "Young men, my suitors now that the great Odysseus has perished, wait, though you are eager to marry me, until I finish this web, so that my weaving will not be useless and wasted. This is a shroud for the hero Laertes, for when the destructive doom of death, which lays men low, shall take him, lest any Achaian woman in this neighborhood hold it against me that a man of many conquests lies with no sheet to wind him."

So she spoke, and the proud heart in us was persuaded. Thereafter in the daytime she would weave at her great loom, but in the night she would have torches set by, and undo it. So for three years she was secret in her design, convincing the Achaians, but when the fourth year came, with the seasons returning, and the months waned, and many days had been brought to completion, one of her women, who knew the whole of the story, told us, and we found her in the act of undoing her glorious weaving. So, against her will and by force, she had to finish it. Then she displayed the great piece of weaving that she had woven. She had washed it and it shone like the sun or the moon. – *The Odyssey of Homer* Trans., Richard Lattimore. (New York: Harper and Row, 1963, 1967. Rpt., 1977), XXIV, 129-148

No matter that Penelope was eventually forced to finish her weaving: by then the story was over. Her role in it had been to personify constancy, faithfulness, prudence, and resourcefulness. Moreover, she found a technique of passive resistance for deflecting the attacks by the suitors on her marriage and the kingdom. So she, too, undergoes a siege, one that echoes her husband's siege of Troy (and Poseidon's siege of him). Troy fell because of Odysseus' cunning and skill; Penelope is forced to capitulate because of her servant's selfishness and stupidity. Penelope personifies waiting as the isometric modality of being.

Another significant difference between our rival patronesses: Arachne entered a contest, the outcome (win or lose) uncertain. Penelope, on the other hand, knows the future (Odysseus will return eventually); she decides to concern herself with the present, with defending and preserving a citadel, and with preserving a state of suspension. Besides, a spider's web has a focus or center; a net does not.

Let Arachne, then, serve as patroness and guide to those nomadic hunters who wander or surf the webs and nets. She spins tales and casts eloquent images to seize the gaze and stun her prey. She is the huntress and the patroness of those who would seek to exploit the net for a goal, profit. She is the left side of the brain on the net; Penelope is the right side. Let Penelope reign as patroness of this new state itself, not a city-state but a global state with the gossipaceous character of a small village, even as the kingdom of Ithaka was small, but no less royal. Urban and orbal.

Finally, what is the significance of what Penelope was doing – weaving a shroud? In the *Odyssey*, she is weaving it for Laertes, son of Arkesios and father of her husband, Odysseus. Laertes, brought back to life by Athena, fought in the last battle in the story (XXIV, 513-525). Fighting alongside his son, he throws the last spear with deadly accuracy and force.

Today, once again, Penelope weaves her shroud, a shroud for the growing millions of disembodied users of the net. This shroud enfolds the world, the World Wide Shroud. And it is never finished, just like the essay thrown out on the net which the author and readers can tinker with, and elaborate on, and comment on, and undo and redo endlessly. And it resembles the net itself, which also shrinks by night and expands by day. The net and the web are themselves encyclopedias, culture-poems of corporate – anonymous, unanimous – authorship.

So today we find ourselves in just such a mythic world of encyclopedic simultaneity: the net and web yield at every moment the living circle of cliché human knowledge, not the shop-worn one-thing-at-a-time narrative laden with archetypes. Our mode now has to be epic, not lyric or dramatic. Not tragic (for finding a private identity), but instead decidedly comic, for the job facing us is that of the beachhead, that of founding a community.

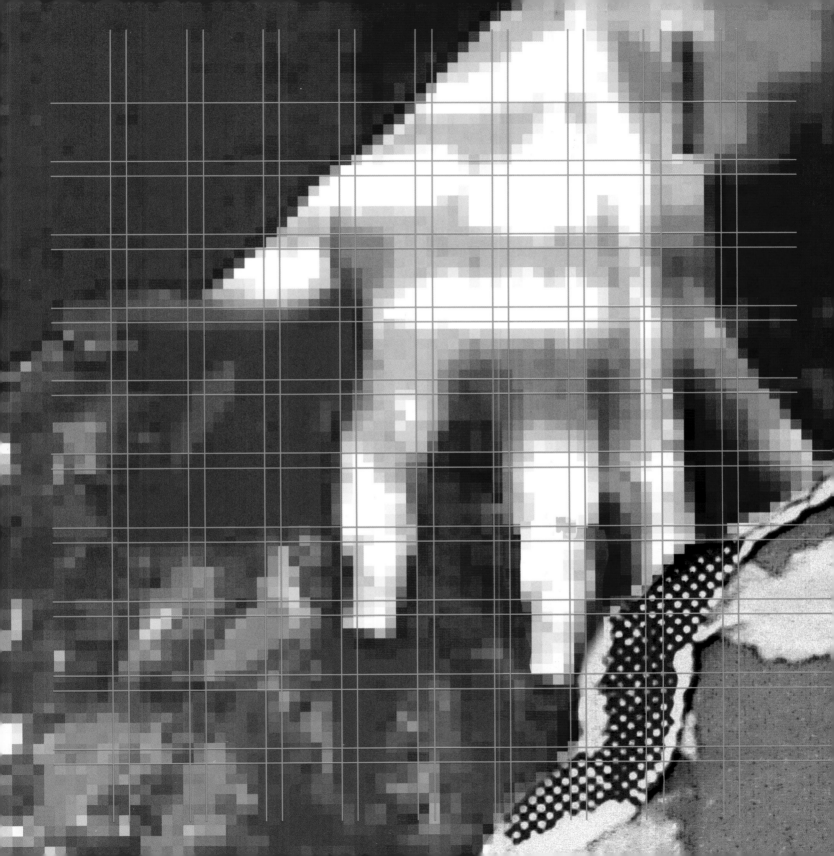

VIRTUAL REALITY

The promoters of Virtual Reality have a novel problem: they can't tell you what it is. Yet sales, and interest, and applications, increase daily...

"I can't tell you what this thing is I'm selling you," reports one huckster.

"That does tend to complicate the problem of sales a bit.

MIME

But there's mileage in the mysteriousness.

WITHOUT

And cutting-edge graphics and more sophisticated 3D simulations are making this supervideogame all the current rage."

WALLS

what is going on here?

The moment you don the VR helmet you shut out the "outside world" and all it implies, and you turn your gaze inward. VR turns the interior landscape into a form of theater.

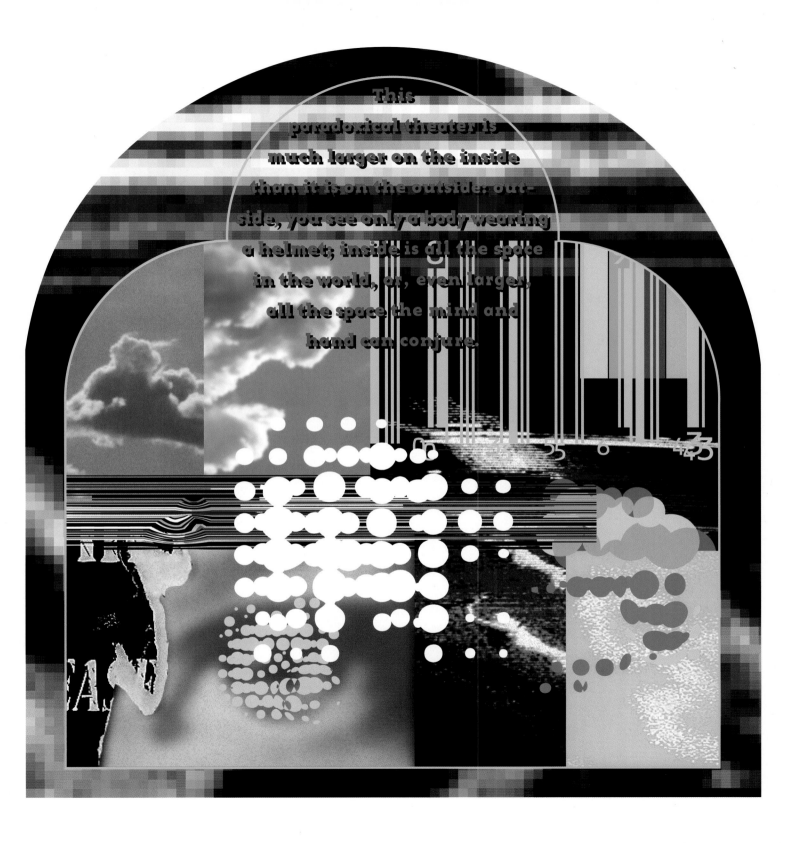

This
paradoxical theater is
much larger on the inside
than it is on the outside: outside, you see only a body wearing
a helmet; inside is all the space
in the world, or, even larger,
all the space the mind and
hand can conjure.

This peculiar theater admits no spectator audience: it has only participants. In that way it resembles Bucky Fuller's idea of Spaceship Earth where there are no passengers, only crew.

VR takes place entirely inside the mind of the user: outer experience and reference points are useless and pointless. The body, as our link to physical reality, and its limitations and propensities, is set aside. Philosophically, the difference could not be more profound: you have just moved from the world of physics – physical reality – into that of metaphysics. VR alters the ground-rules of being and becoming.

The kind of space used in VR is not visual, rational space: it is neither abstract, immutable Newtonian 3-space, nor a static container of objects. The VR user makes this space from moment to moment using gesture and movement, so this space is mutable and responsive to the position and posture of the user. That said, then the VR user is denied having a point of view. Only an observer, someone outside, can have a point of view on any thing or event. The VR user is in a multidimensional, multisensory space compounded of poise and movement and gesture.

Haptic perception involves that melange of senses we lump together under the category of "touch," but haptic is not strictly tactile in the same way one's fingertips convey tactile information about the outside world; rather, haptic tasks like landing a fish or docking a molecule also use the body's internal sense of proprioception that informs us about the position of our own limbs in relation to one another and to thespace around us.

Human proprioception includes a system of internal sensors at joints and in muscles to detect changes in pressure and position. A higher-level processing system detects significant patterns among the body's proprioceptors (e.g., this pattern of messages from this particular set of sensors means that your body is going to topple forward if you don't do something about it; that pattern of messages means that you are pushing something heavy and polished across a low-friction surface). Proprioception's third information system consists of the effectors for transmitting commands from the sensing and sense-making systems to the muscles – the microadjustments that keep us upright and guide our movements. Part of daily life that is so ordinary we hardly notice it is the fast, silent, information-processing and fine muscular coordina-tion skill that enables you to move your hand in exactly the right direction when you decide to reach for a glass of water. A ballet dancer is a virtuoso of proprioception. Haptics involves both proprioceptive and tactile senses, in concert with other senses. – Howard Rheingold, *Virtual Reality* (New York: Summit Books, Simon & Schuster, 1991), pp. 27-28

Because haptic space is space made by the user from moment to moment, wherever you are at any time is the center and the whole focus of the space. So there is no vanishing point, no perspective, no chiaroscuro or foreshortening. The user is the focus: it isn't so much that the user employs all points of view at once as that the user is *looked at* in this haptic space from all points of view at once. In this space, everything is related to everything and to the user and the user's responses – a condition most cultures label paranoia.

What exactly does VR do with the senses? There are several main considerations. First, the helmet cuts off outer vision, so the play in this theater is inside, on the interior landscape. Next, the eyes are separated. This is enormously significant in terms of evolution: each eye is given its own screen to look at, and the two are not allowed to converge. Each eye examines its own world. In evolutionary terms, this gives the user the kind of vision used by fish: each eye "does its own thing" and they never converge on the same thing at the same time, stereoscopically. Actually, although the images presented do simulate binocular 3D, the effect of separating the eyes is really to make the user double-monocular. Because the eyes never converge on an object, as they would in the outer world, the effect is to keep the

visual sense in low definition, subordinate to the other senses. The one-eyed man is the hunter: VR parodies that hunter sensibility: it does not extend the visual, bureaucratic mentality. VR is for hunting and discovery. It is not a visual medium but a proprioceptive one.

Thirdly, the near-point
distance (the distance between
the eye and the thing observed) in the
helmet is some four inches or less, so no
"hard focus" convergence would be possible in
any case. When reading, for example, if the page is
three or four inches from the eyes, both eyes cannot
converge so one eye – first one then the other –
shuts off and the reader operates monocularly.
Eventually, one of the reader's eyes takes over and
the other idles, resulting in a strong eye and a
weak eye. Literacy calls for convergence and
intellectual as well as physical distance
and detachment. If VR uses a distance
inhospitable to literacy,

those who find
the experience of its distances
congenial are by so much alienated
from literacy. Under the circumstances
provided by VR, the eye reverts to "soft focus"
and looks through a screen rather than at
things. This is to bring back into play the sensory
modes of the early middle ages, modes that prevailed
before the invention of visual or pictorial space.
For the haptic VR user does not perform in an
abstract space so much as a fluid one that he
makes and conjures from moment to moment.
It has no single outside point of view or
point of reference; it has in fact
no outside.

"Imagine immersing yourself in an artificial world and actively exploring it, rather than peering in at it from a fixed perspective through a flat screen in a movie theater, on a television set, or on a computer display. Imagine that you are the creator as well as the consumer of your artificial experience, with the power to use a gesture or word to remold the world you see and hear and feel. That part is not fiction. The head-mounted displays (HMDs) and three-dimensional computer graphics, input/output devices, computer models that constitute a VR system make it possible, today, to immerse yourself in an artificial world and to reach in and reshape it" (Rheingold, *Op.Cit.*, p. 16).

Under conditions of such profound
involvement as the Internet and VR afford,
private, individual identity is irrelevant
as well as being impossible to sustain.
Private individualism calls for great
intellectual detachment of knower
from known, and abstraction in
the very process of knowing.
Participation is incommensurate
with private identity.

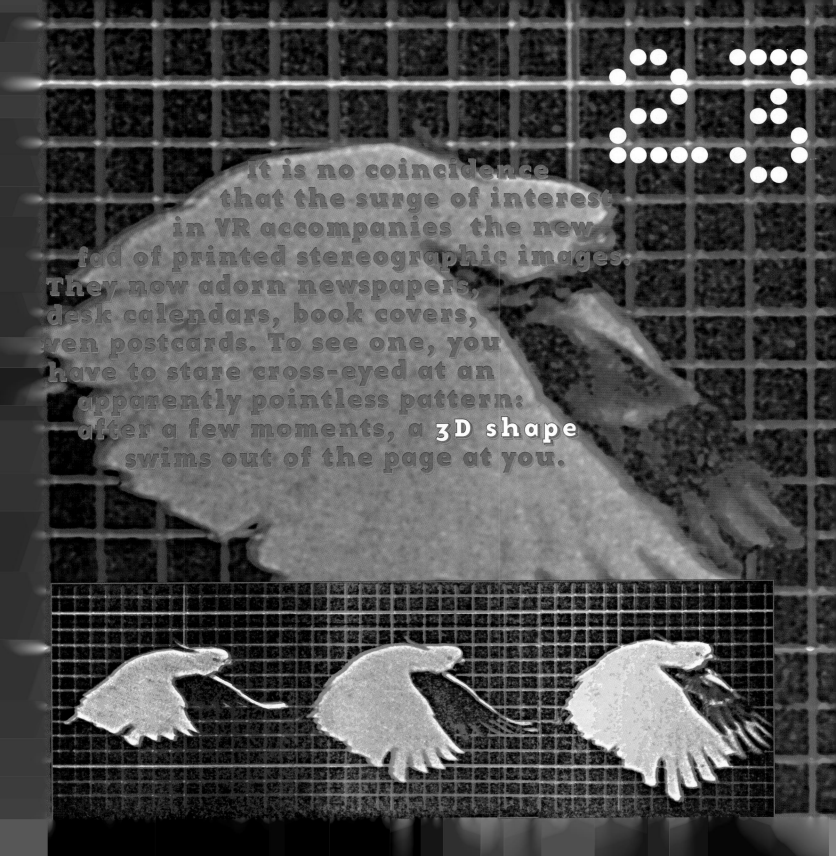

It is no coincidence
that the surge of interest
in VR accompanies the new
fad of printed stereographic images.
They now adorn newspapers,
desk calendars, book covers,
even postcards. To see one, you
have to stare cross-eyed at an
apparently pointless pattern:
after a few moments, a **3D shape**
swims out of the page at you.

That children find it easy to see these images while adults find them difficult indicates that the adults still have some lingering, residual visual bias from the habits of alphabetic literacy which does not impede their postliterate children. These images (and VR) use the same method of soft focus: the convergence point for the eyes is some inches away from the surface of the page (below it for a convex image or above it for a concave image). With these images, there is no fixed point of view, no use of perspective or vanishing points or chiaroscuro. In brief, no objective "truth": because the viewer is co-creator and has to change, to adapt his or her senses to meet the image halfway in order to be able to "see" it, the viewer has surrendered the possibility of detachment or objectivity.

You have to move about to navigate in the "Virtual World": you don't sit there with a channel changer or tap at a keypad. Mime, the art most closely associated with VR and body movement, holds the key to the new virtual worlds: you mime your way around in the virtual space, a space either generated by or responsive to the user's postures and gestures. If this new toy soon takes a serious place in the world of science or of art, it will be because the disciplines developed in mime have already mapped all of the virtual spaces imaginable. Corporal mime, which reaches back to preliteracy, will provide the avant-garde cyberpunk's bodily discipline and asceticism.

Describe to a doctor the symptoms of TV-watching. "Doc, I have this friend: he sits for hours at a time staring at a pane of glass. He doesn't move but sits relaxed in a recliner or on a couch. He just keeps staring; his eyes barely flicker and his blink rate is down," and so on. Ask the doctor for a diagnosis of the condition and you will be told, "The person you describe is hypnotized" – a reasonably accurate diagnosis.

Now describe the symptoms of VR. "Doc, my friend stands in a bit of a crouch and doesn't attend to anything or anyone in front of him. He shuffles about with one or both hands groping aimlessly in the air; he waves one hand about and points with it and mutters spasmodically..."

Have you seen people doing this on the street, in RL (the computerati's way of referring to Real Life)? What do you call it?

Virtual Reality [Effect of circuitry: dramatizes wired world]

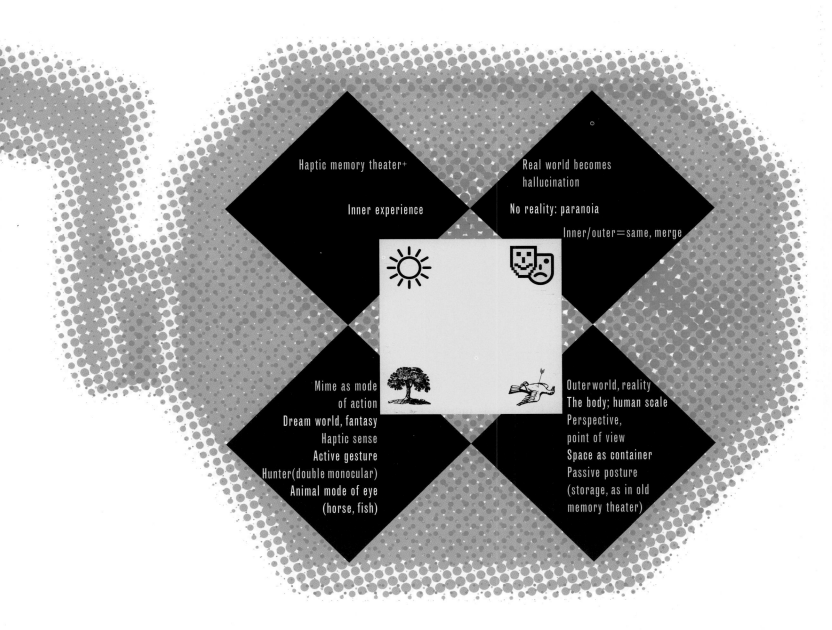

Haptic memory theater+

Inner experience

Real world becomes
hallucination

No reality: paranoia

Inner/outer=same, merge

Mime as mode
of action
Dream world, fantasy
Haptic sense
Active gesture
Hunter(double monocular)
Animal mode of eye
(horse, fish)

Outerworld, reality
The body; human scale
Perspective,
point of view
Space as container
Passive posture
(storage, as in old
memory theater)

+ The old Western rhetorical science of trained memory used imaginary "memory theaters." You carried in your head detailed images of houses and castles and rooms. Entire buildings would serve as filing cabinets to store the things you wanted to remember. You made the images on the fly. You enter the imagined building and on the coat rack on your right in the vestibule you place the first thing you want to retrieve later. You imagine in exact photographic detail the item you placed on the rack. It uses posture: remember where (configurationally) you left it.

This kind of memory theater is not static but moving: you tour the place as you stow the goods, and you tour the place as you retrieve them. By contrast, the VR memory theater uses active gesture. You mime your way around.

A Word About Tetrads

Every medium, every human innovation, has a linguistic structure. Our media endlessly translate and distort their contents and users alike into new forms and postures. The media are active forms, not passive containers.

As we accelerate the pace of invention, it becomes increasingly evident that media themselves are not only languages but also words in a language of forms (of communication). We are now producing – uttering – new media and devices with ever-greater rapidity; this accelerating speech of ours causes "backward" cultures around the world both fascination and deep concern. While we fall under the spell of these novelties, they see how easily our technologies distort or wipe out centuries-old patterns of society. As the pace increases, so does the need to anticipate effects before releasing a new medium into a culture.

Media penetrate and modify human cultures in much the same way that viruses attack and alter organic ones. In periods when change occurs slowly, it is possible to control or to adapt to the new situation. We had thousands of years to accustom ourselves to manuscript culture, and the age of print lasted from the fifteenth century to our own. The telegraph age lasted until radio: two to three generations. Presently, the interval between revolutions is not generations but two or three years – which allows no time for adjustment. The pace has exceeded human capacity to absorb and adjust.

Every word in every spoken language is a metaphor.

The word for something is not itself the thing named, but it is a way to experience it, a "way of seeing" or of knowing the thing. So any and every word translates experience from one form (direct sensation) to another (verbal sensation). So metaphors have four parts, and media equally have four constant dimensions. Just as the parts of a good metaphor are in balance with respect to each other, so too are the four dimensions of our media and technologies. In that way, too, our technologies are words and speech.

Every innovation enlarges or amplifies some area of sensibility or experience or action; when that process is pushed far enough it will reverse its characteristics and a complementary process will take over. And every innovation simultaneously displaces some facet of current action or experience, even as it reintroduces some long-forgotten facet. These four processes occur in every case. Moreover, they apply *exclusively* to human activities and innovations.[*]

True, every one of our innovations has a great many effects and side-effects, many of them unexpected. But since only these four apply in every case without exception, they afford a certain means of prediction. A "tetrad" is a formal statement about some innovation that shows its pattern of these four effects. When exploring the matter, it generally helps to state the four effects, the four "parts" of the tetrad, as questions. "Parts" understood as in a choir – part-singing, voices – because they are simultaneous. Like voices in a choir, at any moment in the music one voice or another may dominate the attention or be carrying the melody while the others work below the surface; in the music of media, all four are always present.

[*] For a full discussion of these four transformations and their meaning, see *Laws of Media: The New Science* by Marshall and Eric McLuhan, University of Toronto Press, 1988.

The four processes operate simultaneously: there is no sequence of them. All four inhabit each and every human innovation from the first moment it appears. For that reason they are set down together to reinforce the idea of simultaneity and to bypass the temptation to impose a sequence on them.

The four processes are presented as four chunks of information – a chunk at each of the corners of an imaginary square. The icons that identify the chunks appear at the core rather than at the outer corners. Like this:

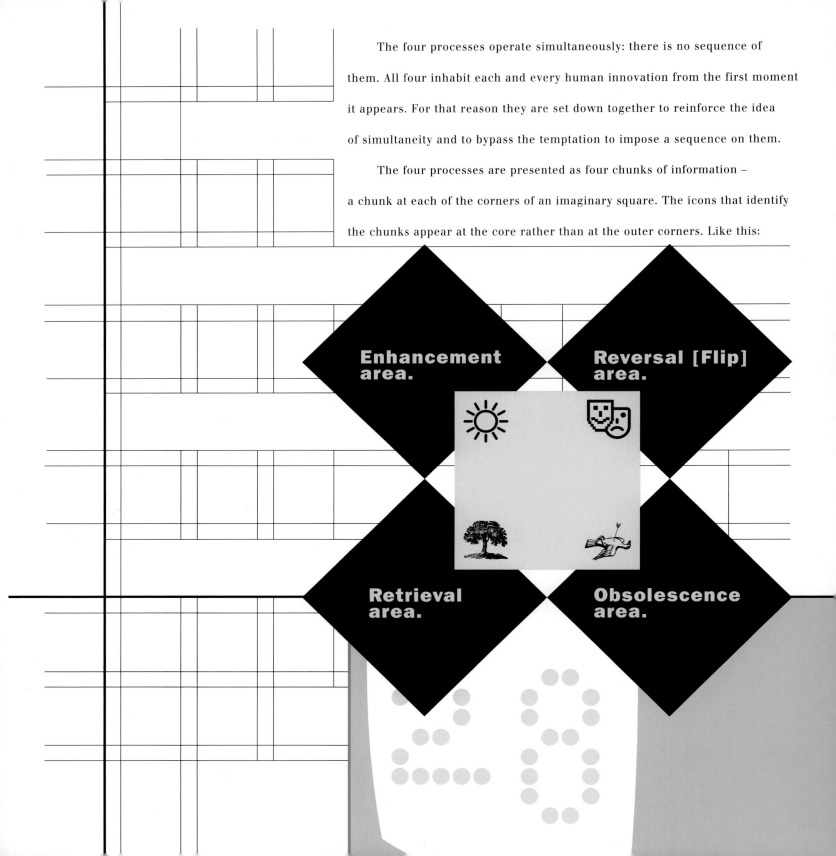

Enhancement area.

Reversal [Flip] area.

Retrieval area.

Obsolescence area.

The icon below stands for the process of enhancing.

One of the parts: what is **Enhanced**, that is, enlarged, amplified, or increased (or miniaturized) or accelerated (if previously slow) or retarded (if previously fast) etc.? Several examples:

• Humor / joking / wit enhance playfulness

• The car and plane vastly accelerate the speed of travel, enhance mobility

• Inoculation triggers immunity

• Print enhances uniformity of the text

• Money/uniform currency speeds transactions

• Xerox speeds the copying process, enlarges the ease of duplication

• The Pill makes the user infallible, machine-like

• Virtual Reality amplifies the imaginary, fantasy world, the inner world

• Street-parking permits enhance the issuer's control over license to park

• Pizza: enhances plain food, satura, variety, mix

• E-mail enhances 1-to-1 contact, speed of access, convenience

• Murphy's Law spotlights perversity, grievance, luck

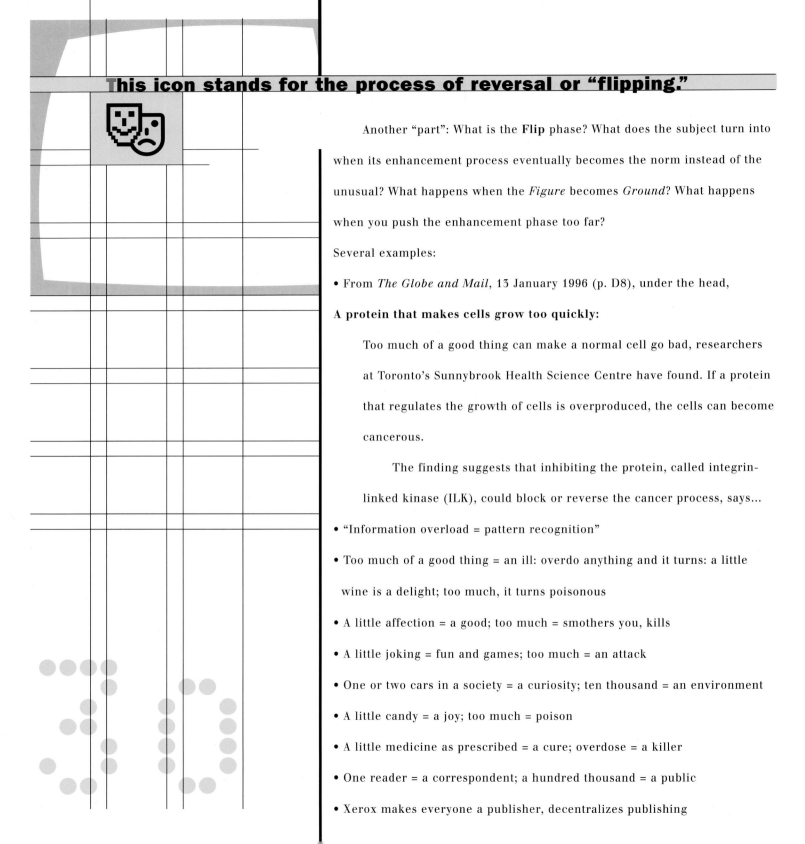

Another "part": What is the **Flip** phase? What does the subject turn into when its enhancement process eventually becomes the norm instead of the unusual? What happens when the *Figure* becomes *Ground*? What happens when you push the enhancement phase too far?

Several examples:

• From *The Globe and Mail*, 13 January 1996 (p. D8), under the head,

A protein that makes cells grow too quickly:

> Too much of a good thing can make a normal cell go bad, researchers at Toronto's Sunnybrook Health Science Centre have found. If a protein that regulates the growth of cells is overproduced, the cells can become cancerous.
>
> The finding suggests that inhibiting the protein, called integrin-linked kinase (ILK), could block or reverse the cancer process, says...

• "Information overload = pattern recognition"

• Too much of a good thing = an ill: overdo anything and it turns: a little wine is a delight; too much, it turns poisonous

• A little affection = a good; too much = smothers you, kills

• A little joking = fun and games; too much = an attack

• One or two cars in a society = a curiosity; ten thousand = an environment

• A little candy = a joy; too much = poison

• A little medicine as prescribed = a cure; overdose = a killer

• One reader = a correspondent; a hundred thousand = a public

• Xerox makes everyone a publisher, decentralizes publishing

Another "part": What now turns **Obsolescent**? What is displaced? Pushed off stage or out of the spotlight? What gets sidelined while the enhancement process gets under way? What *used to be* the norm (but is no longer as a result of the new thing)? Sometimes this process drives the whole set of relationships. This year's model car deliberately makes last year's obsolete. Nothing is as obsolete as yesterday's newspaper or last week's ad campaign. What used to be "in charge" before the novelty arrived? Several examples:

- Humor, joking, wit banish melancholy, sternness, sobriety

- The PC obsolesced the secretary

- Radio obsolesced the music hall and concert hall

- TV obsolesced Hollywood and its theater chains and its star system

- The newspaper obsolesced the book as a form of news

- Print obsolesced medieval manuscript culture, the scribes and scriptoria

- The alphabet obsolesced the power of the bards

- Money obsolesced barter

- Virtual Reality obsolesces the outer world

- Inoculation obsolesces the need to suffer the disease, the threat

- The Pill banishes human fallibility

- Romanticism sidesteps rationalist sensibility

- Virtual reality makes the outside world, the "real world" irrelevant

- E-mail: obsolesces snail mail, telephone call, visit, couriers, formality

- The car obsolesced the horse and the railroad; it obsolesced the centralized city

Another "part": What is **Renewed? Retrieved? Reactivated?**

What old – perhaps *very* old – thing is updated here? What comeback is made? What is revived? Revivals and retrievals occur conspicuously in culture and the arts, but also in the sciences and elsewhere. Lately, for example, we have seen a rash of old TV shows reappearing as feature movies: *Batman, Mission: Impossible, The Fugitive*. The old thing comes back, but always in a new form and on a new ground – renewed, with new aesthetic significance.

Several examples:

• Humor, joking retrieve life, sanity, health

• Print brought back the manuscripts of antiquity

• The car and motorcycle bring back the knight in shining armor;
   they retrieve the road and turnpike and toll road as highways

• TV brings back the movie and turns it into an art form, an aesthetic activity

• The movie retrieves the novel

• The computer makes old TV shows retrievable as new aesthetic forms:
   Mission: Impossible, The Fugitive, Superman

• Speech retrieves thought

• The WWW and the Internet retrieve the oral encyclopedia of the preliterate,
   pre-Homeric poets

• Chaos theory retrieves order in large systems

• Rock music retrieves the amateur musician, the small group

• Rap music retrieves *recitativo secco*

• Inoculation retrieves the disease in harmless form (dead)

- The digital watch retrieves the sundial (uses light to tell time)

- Virtual Reality retrieves mime as its mode of operation, retrieves the interior landscape as the stage

- Money retrieves goods in uniform mode for uniform pricing

- Xerox retrieves the oral committee (position papers)

- Street-parking permit: retrieves the orderly neighborhood

- E-mail retrieves oral chattiness, extreme sensitivity (RH), retrieves the teletype machine in a new form, informality, immediacy

- Murphy's Law retrieves the irrational explanation, perverse cosmos, inevitability

A few examples from the above

First, humor, joking, wittiness.

12345

Enhances playfulness

A little = fun and games;
Too much = an attack

Restores life,
sanity,
health

Banishes melancholy,
sterness, sobriety,
severity

Second, let's try it on pizza. In the sixties, pizza arrived on these shores as exotic European food; it was – to the North American palate of the time – spicy and exotic. (To the Europeans and Italians, it was just another way to make use of leftovers: everyday fare.)

Enhances plain food, variety, mix

Flips into fancy snob fare: "gourmet pizza"; what began as spicy and exotic turns into bland uniformity

Retrieves the leftovers

Pushes aside formality, leisure, blue- or red-ribbon chef; home-cooked dinners; other take-out food or other instant foods

As a third example, let us try a technology from the list: **speech.**

Speech enhances articulation, expression

Reversal: slowed down, becomes song; In excess, turns to verbosity and noise, prattle

Speech retrieves thought, knits community

Banishes silence, communication by grunt, gesture, sign

Another technology: **Xeroxing (photocopying).**

Speeds the copying
process
enlarges ease of dupication

Makes everyone
a publisher
decentralizes publishing

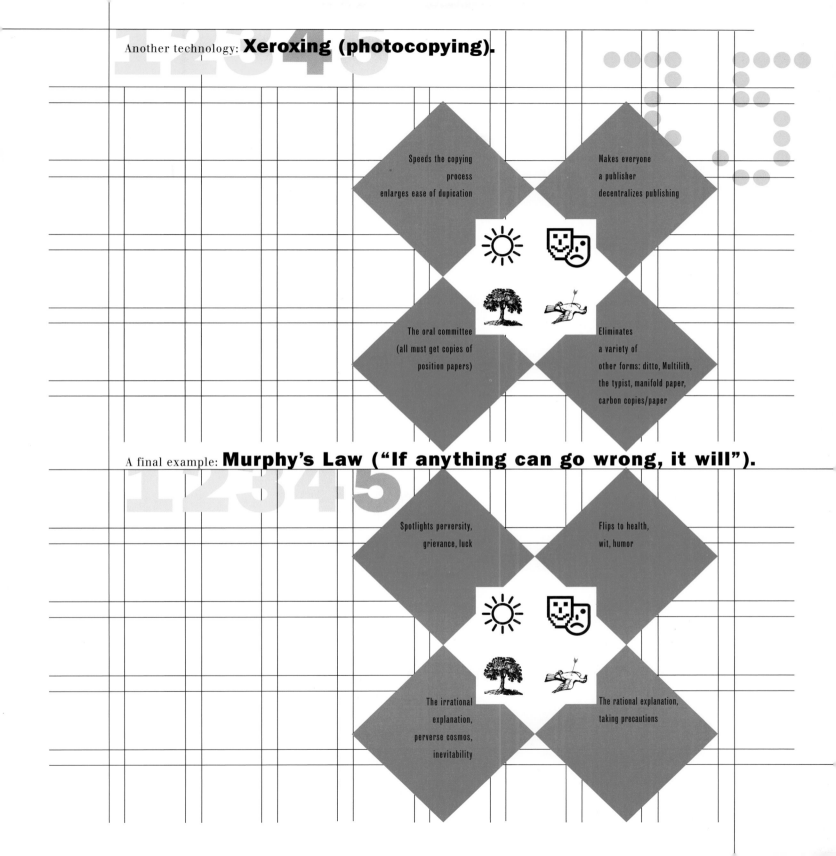

The oral committee
(all must get copies of
position papers)

Eliminates
a variety of
other forms: ditto, Multilith,
the typist, manifold paper,
carbon copies/paper

A final example: **Murphy's Law ("If anything can go wrong, it will").**

Spotlights perversity,
grievance, luck

Flips to health,
wit, humor

The irrational
explanation,
perverse cosmos,
inevitability

The rational explanation,
taking precautions

Rhyme scheme

The four "parts" of a tetrad are like the lines in a stanza of a poem. Here, however, situations and things, rather than words, provide the rhymes.

In a poem, the words' ends echo each other to produce the rhymes. *Late, grate, spate,* and *fate* rhyme and also look alike, as they all end *-ate*. But then *goat* and *rote* rhyme without looking alike, and so do *too, two, to, shoe, blue,* and *flew.*

In a tetrad, with the components arranged as above, each "part" or cluster of ideas displays an ongoing process or situation. Instead of similar sounds, then, you look for other kinds of similarities. Similar forms. Formal relations, formal resonance.

You will discover a sort of theme common, say, to the items along the top, and a complementary one among the items along the bottom. The top, for example, may be concerned with groups and the bottom with individuals. For example, in the tetrad on Teleconferencing (p. 57), the top concerns, among other things, role playing in business and in politics; the bottom, the effect of the technology on proxemic distances and on the senses involved.

In the tetrad on Electric Crowds (p. 158), the top discusses interior awareness; the bottom, exterior or outer awareness.

Similarly, in a finished tetrad, the left side will exhibit a common theme, as it were, and the right side a complementary one. The right side may be concerned with things that are orderly and the left with things that are disorderly or anarchical. For example, in the tetrad on Virtual Reality (p. 25), the left side emphasizes the effects of that technology on the inner world; the right side, the effects of the outer or "real" world. In the one on the Telephone (p. 158), the left side discusses mimesis or making processes; the right, mirroring and matching processes.

A tetrad takes a fair bit of "tuning" of that sort to get it polished. In the same manner, the words in a poem have to be shuffled and tuned to get the rhymes right, all the while working to keep the ideas and the sense intact. And, as poets have often observed, the tuning process often reveals unexpected things about the subject: poets admit that they often get some of their best ideas while looking for rhymes. If the "rhymes" are not quite right, neither are the ideas. And new ideas and fresh discoveries are often found while fine-tuning (looking for rhymes). The same is true of our tetrads. Mind and ear must harmonize: the information has to be accurate, and yet the "rhyming" must be true.

We encounter similar four-part relations every day in an informal way. For example, among the inside blurbs in a recent novel (*Kiss the Girls* by James Patterson), we find this: "James Patterson is to suspense what Danielle Steel is to romance." A is to B as C is to D. Or,

| Patterson | is to | suspense |
| Steele | is to | romance |

Is it reversible? Can it be arranged A is to C as B is to D? That is, instead of reading the four elements horizontally, can they be "read" vertically? That would produce "James Patterson is to Danielle Steel what suspense is to romance." Has the writer's intention been preserved? Do the relations hold? In this case it seems a bit extreme, but it works – in a way.

Here is another example from the same source: "Robert B. Parker's Spenser, Patricia Cornwell's Kay Scarpetta, and Evan Hunter's 87th Precinct detectives..." This sets up a trio of pairs: Parker is to his hero, Spenser, as Cornwell is to her Scarpetta, as Hunter is to the 87th Precinct detectives... One component is the writer; the other, the character. Writer is to writer is to writer as character is to character is to character. Or writer is to character, as writer is to character, as writer is to character.

"Parking tickets are to couriers what fleas are to dogs." Well enough. But how about this: "Parking tickets are to couriers what dogs are to postmen"? In that case, isn't one part of the example too extreme? Couriers find parking tickets an annoyance, an irritation; but postmen are often seriously threatened by dogs. So the first set works; the second has flaws.

Try a few more:

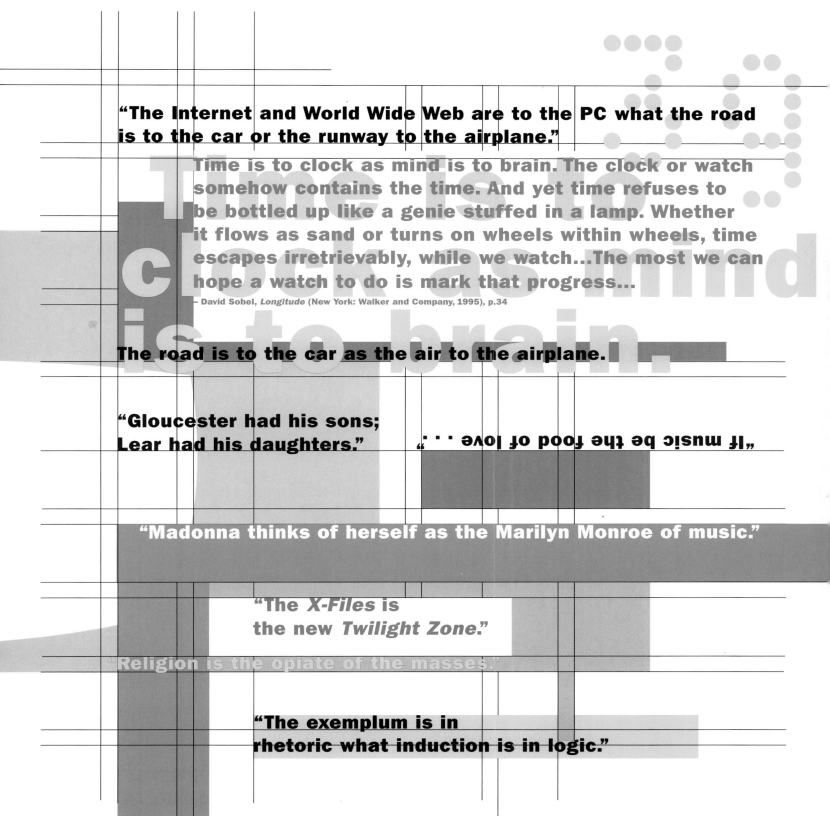

"The Internet and World Wide Web are to the PC what the road is to the car or the runway to the airplane."

Time is to clock as mind is to brain. The clock or watch somehow contains the time. And yet time refuses to be bottled up like a genie stuffed in a lamp. Whether it flows as sand or turns on wheels within wheels, time escapes irretrievably, while we watch...The most we can hope a watch to do is mark that progress...

– David Sobel, *Longitude* (New York: Walker and Company, 1995), p.34

The road is to the car as the air to the airplane.

"Gloucester had his sons;
Lear had his daughters."

"If music be the food of love . . ."

"Madonna thinks of herself as the Marilyn Monroe of music."

"The *X-Files* is
the new *Twilight Zone*."

"Religion is the opiate of the masses."

"The exemplum is in
rhetoric what induction is in logic."

When composing tetrads, take care not to mix or blend incongruous levels of action. For example, Christmas and Easter: Can Santa Claus be to Christmas what the Easter Bunny is to Easter?

Santa Claus	is to	Christmas (what the)
Easter Bunny	is to	Easter

Read the same relations vertically instead of horizontally: Santa Claus is to the Easter Bunny as Christmas is to Easter. The relation holds.

Now try a different level, say, that of the *meaning* of the feasts / holidays: Birth is to Christmas what re-birth, or the Resurrection, is to Easter.

Birth	Christmas
Resurrection (re-birth)	Easter

And read vertically instead of horizontally:

Birth	is to	Resurrection as
Christmas	is to	Easter.

That works, too, in its way.

But blend the two levels and chaos results: Birth is to Resurrection as Santa is to the Easter Bunny. The result is comic and patently idiotic. Although each pair (Santa / Bunny, and birth / Resurrection) works well enough with the common pair (Christmas / Easter), they clearly function at very different levels. One is not wrong and the other right: both are right, each in its own way. Each is a dimension of the Christmas / Easter relationship. One concerns events in this world; the other, those in the next.

So in a tetrad. There may often be several levels going at the same time: keep them separate. To begin with, however, just jot down everything you can find or think of; later, sort what you have into groups and levels.

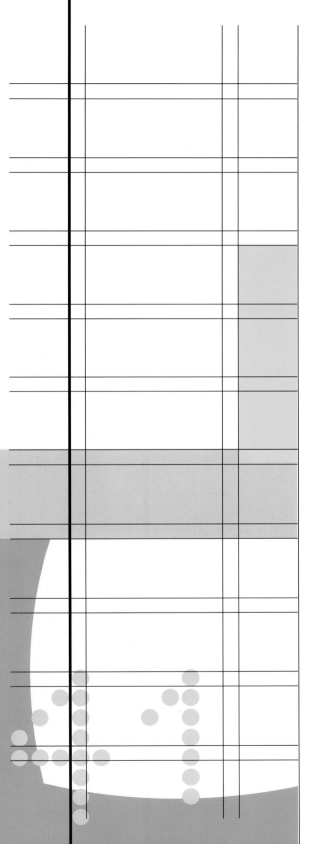

The four corners, when the tetrad is tuned aright (and that sometimes takes quite a lot of doing), will be in the relation, A is to B as C is to D. The traditional name for this "ratio among ratios" is "proper proportion."

The ratios that the tetrad shows up regarding how our artifacts operate give much more than an odd coincidence: they serve a practical purpose.

As in math, so in culture and technology: when you have three of the four you know automatically an enormous amount about the missing element. Given "X is to three as 4 is to six," finding X presents little difficulty. Or,

X : 3 = 4 : 6,

also written as

$$\frac{x}{3} = \frac{4}{6}$$

and the same equation read horizontally instead of vertically,

$$\frac{x}{4} = \frac{3}{6}$$

The resonant pattern means you can not only cross-check each element but also identify missing ones, so the tetrad can also help with prediction. Again, four general statements are true of all human artifacts, without exception. Not a single case has yet been found where only three apply (though often it takes a while to locate one or another).

The four parts of the tetrad provide just a starting point for investigation; they are not the end of the search but the beginning. Still, it can be useful, when beginning an investigation, to know that the subject will definitely pass along four roads, that there are four specific and reliable places to look to find what it holds in store.

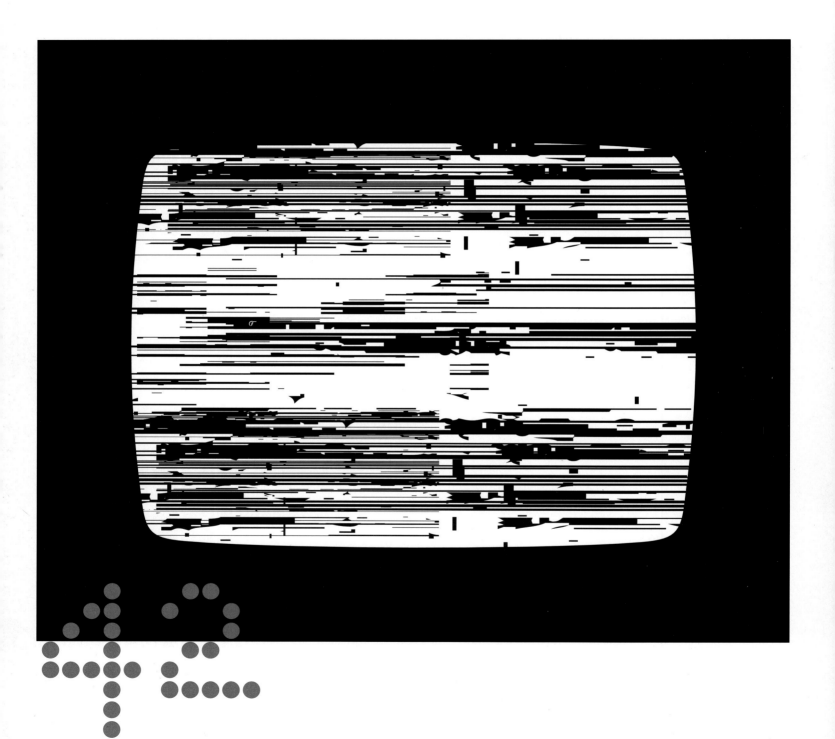

TELECONFERENCING:
THE
GLOBAL
THEATER

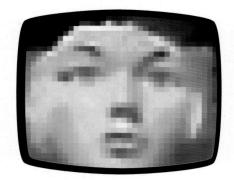

International teleconferencing turns the global village created by radio into a global theater – a theater of the absurd.
This new form of theatrics uses no plot or script, only role-playing and participation. Nor does it have an audience,
such as you would expect to find in an ordinary theater. The moment spectators are added, the action converts into a
performance. Without spectators, without an audience, any theatrical production just as much as a football game turns
into a practice session, a rehearsal. (Just imagine the effect of adding a theater-style audience to the boardroom antics
of a teleconference.) Teleconferences have a closer relation to actors' workshops or the familiar talk show: instead
of a script, there is an agenda or set of themes for ad-libbing. The teleconference puts the boardroom inside another
situation: doing so makes the old boardroom itself obsolete and turns it into a stage.

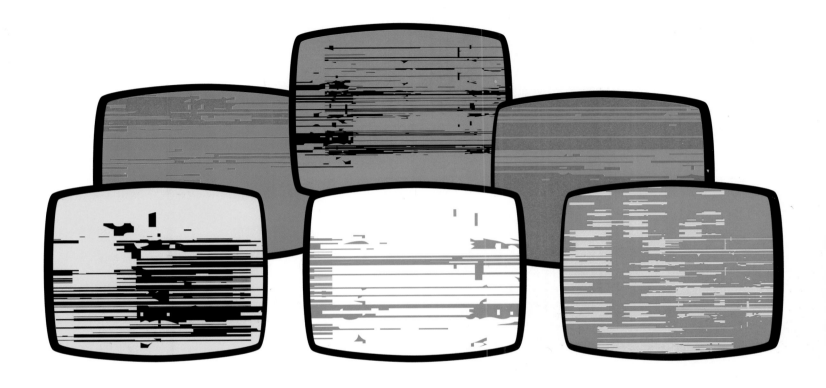

Power, in this video medium, issues from the better image, the one with the most charisma – a circumstance familiar to politicians and to professional actors and actresses. Politicians have learned that power is no longer related to policies and platforms, but comes from their ability to manipulate images. Charisma and imagery cannot be quantified and have no relation to bottom-line measurability: charisma is the ability to put on – to "identify with" – a large audience. The larger the group, the greater the power. The shift is from substance to style, from left side of the brain to right, from concepts and ideology to perception. As a new member of the video family, frequent teleconferencing will transform the nature of power in the corporate environment as surely as television transformed the nature of power in culture and politics and the (video) desk-top computer or word-processor transformed the nature of the office work and the balance of the sexes.

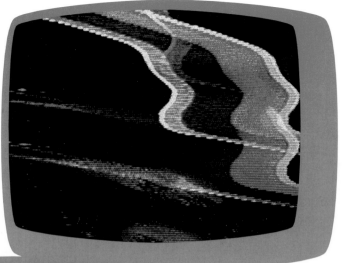

Television wrecked Hollywood and the star system on which it was built, not because of the smaller screen or the small "inconvenience" of having to go out to a theater, but because it changed the user. Hollywood began a program of intense experimentation the moment television appeared on the scene, introducing wrap-around screens, 3-D, color, stereo sound – all in direct response to the new sensibility brought into play by TV. People accustomed to TV demanded far greater psychic and sensory involvement than Hollywood, accustomed to an audience schooled in radio and the press, knew how to provide. Only the elderly now remember the old star system: film stars were treated like visiting royalty. Thousands would turn out to greet visiting stars at the airport; they were mobbed at public appearances and at movie premieres. Mayors turned out to present them the keys to the city. No such red-carpet treatment follows the appearance in your neighborhood of a TV newscaster or host. On TV, there are just "TV personalities." People don't act on TV, they behave. The same will soon be true of this new extension of the medium of television: there are no great stars, just polished personae and great committees.

Teleconferencing does not exist in a vacuum, but against a largely invisible *ground* of related and supporting services and activities. Much of media study consists in examining the *ground* of any innovation. In fact, the terms

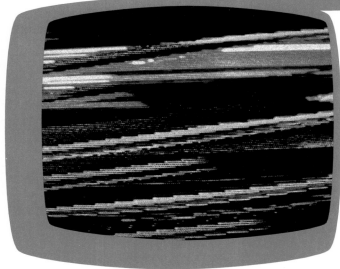

ground and *medium* are largely interchangeable. One part of this *ground* is the pervasive computer screen. When TV was new, people were concerned about sitting too close to the screen: underneath this concern was their realization that objectivity is lost when one gets too close to any event or circumstance. Their kids, however, instinctively sat just a couple of feet from the screen in order to maximize their involvement. They were trying to climb inside the images, put them on, enmesh themselves in them. It was some years before we realized the enormous power of TV to involve in depth any user, regardless of what the user thought of the program. Look today at how close to the same TV screen people sit and work when it sits on their desks and is called a computer monitor.

With a film, at any given moment, the screen presents either a complete photographic image or a blank. The image on the screen is static: there is no movement in a movie, just a quick succession of (in effect) slides and blanks. As with a cartoon strip in the newspaper, all of the movement occurs in the intervals between the frames, and is supplied by the viewer. So it is fair to say that the viewer of a movie has no objectivity; the viewer is denied any possibility of objectivity because he or she has been an intimate and unconscious participant by supplying all of the movement. This condition applies regardless of what the film is about or whether the viewer likes it or not.

With the TV and computer screen, the involvement escalates. At any given moment on the screen there is not a full image or a blank, as with film. The TV screen presents a few dots or a line or two of dots of light in a ceaselessly forming and re-forming mosaic. Given but a few dots here and there, the user supplies from moment to moment all the rest of the image. Second, the light-through screen shines at you, it uses you as the screen: it tattoos the user with images and light. Film pales by comparison, so the studios responded by trying many ways to satisfy the TV-user's need for more involvement. When a film goes on TV it doesn't have the effect of film any more: the succession of static images and blanks is translated into the TV mosaic of dots and now has the effect of TV. It undergoes a translation, as much as does a book or an opera that finds itself on film or a song that finds its way into a book of verse. This shift has little or nothing to do with the size of the page or of the screen (which filmmakers routinely blame when their products fail on TV and never credit when they succeed). It is entirely a matter of how the user's faculties are engaged. The same is true of a teleconference: it will not have the same properties or effect as does the lecture hall or boardroom. In the sixties, "educational TV" failed spectacularly because the classroom repertoire bore no relation to the sensibility of the TV user. Today, movies are made with the realization that their biggest earnings will be made in the home video market, not in theaters, so they are "formatted" - made - to suit TV. Hollywood, like politics, has adapted: so will business and school.

Television has long been derided as the medium of "talking heads." But isn't it natural to use the close-up to simulate proximity for people who crave involvement? The close-up, featuring the head with or without shoulders, provides the *effect* of intimacy. Try this experiment (with someone roughly your height): look at the other person's eyes as you slowly approach until all you can see, in focus and periphery together, is the head and shoulder-tops. Normally, the result is about 3" to 4" nose-to-nose. That, then, is the *effect* of the shot we find most congenial on TV: that is the speaking distance or "comfort zone" of television. It is not the comfort zone of the eye, the distance at which you can see your interlocutor: at 3-4", other senses come into play. In terms of ordinary experience, it is impossible to be polite or civilized with strangers at that distance. (Try it, if you're feeling adventurous.) The preferred distance between people speaking to each other in Western (alphabetic) culture used to be arm's distance, or about three feet. That interval we Westerners traditionally find, or found, congenial for speaking. But according to anthropologists who study these distances, other cultures prefer very different distances. Arabs, for example, liked to be 6" or 8" apart: that distance is an osmic space, an interval in which smell operates comfortably and the nose can sniff and suss-out the other. At three feet, arm's distance, the eye comes into operation easily and the more intimate senses don't work as well. TV is not a visual medium: it does not use the eye as an eye, but as a hand or an ear. It prefers contour and outline to detail, and regards perspective and foreshortening – which go with detachment and objectivity and point of view – as inconsequential.

In addition to extending the body and the sensibilities of the user, every technology brings with it an environment of services and disservices as a side effect – its medium, or *ground*. The medium is invisible because it is ignored, taken for granted. Yet without it the technology could not function. But the invisible medium is the prime agent of transformation. For example, the *ground* of the motor car is principally the road, plus oil and gas supplies (and all the politics that go with them). It also includes all manufacture, design, retail, and reselling, parking lots, service facilities, shopping malls, adjustments to urban design and the creation of suburbs, and rearrangements in lives, leisure and recreation, and business. It makes no difference what the car is used for, moral, immoral, or amoral: without roads and gas and the rest, the car is just an *objet d'art*, a sculptural folly. Needless to say, the *ground* is immeasurably larger than the *figure* that imposes it, and it is in the *ground* that the side-effects occur.

The teleconference must be produced. That is, for more than two users or stations ("multipoint" work), there must be a producer at a switcher, TV-studio-style, "calling the shots." The "set" calls for a dedicated room.

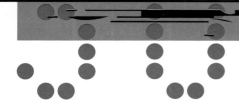

The behind-the-scenes crew, by its existence, converts the conference into theater, the mere meeting into performance and role playing. Thereby, what used to be the "back room" assumes center stage, and the crew and producer become the invisible "back-room boys." The medium is in charge and dictates what can and will occur in it. Additionally, the signal must be transmitted via telephone land lines or satellite or both, so those technologies are also needed as elements of the *ground* for teleconferencing and videoconferencing.

Speaking of telephone lines recalls the unsuccessful attempts by our own telephone companies to market "videophone" or "picturephone," the telephone with a small video screen attached. It never found a market, although the telephone company invested considerable sums in its development and tried mightily to market it. Since we now have a computer hybrid that imitates it – and videoconferencing – in a small way, it might be worthwhile considering why "picturephone" failed. Desktop computers now feature an option of having inset on the screen a TV-style image of an interlocutor while the rest of the screen continues with the usual text and graphics manipulable by both parties.

The telephone, although intimate, was too high-definition an audio form to accommodate the tactile TV image. Consider the interpersonal distance of the ordinary phone call. IN EFFECT, how distant are you from your interlocutor? How far are your lips from his or her ear? A foot or two?

The basic technique for studying a *ground* is inventory. Inventory all of the support structures and side-effects of videoconferencing. What has to be in place in order for the videoconference to be possible or feasible? Here are some of the items to consider.

- The effect on air and other forms of travel, hotels, etc.
- All of the production facilities needed (rooms, equipment, and manufacture and sale of same, including the personnel)
- Land lines and satellites, radio/TV technology, and their manufacture, design, maintenance
- With land lines, the telephone system, *et al.*
- With satellites, space technology, *et al.*
- The very internationality of business, what that implies, how it is affected
- The kind of business dealings that it makes possible
- The kinds of sabotage and industrial espionage available – and not...etc.
- The various nations themselves involved and bypassed
- Ask the same questions with reference to all other users of videoconference: in schools, politics...

An alternate inventory technique for revealing *ground* is to ask this question: What if videoconferencing were suddenly, magically, deleted? What would be affected and to what degree? What activities would cease, return, enlarge, diminish? What other media would be involved to take up the slack?

When the inventories are well under way, the patterns of influence and impact stand out, and some of the nature of the medium clarifies itself. Videoconferencing is still new, and hasn't yet had a very extensive impact: but try the exercise with desktop computers, for example. Or photocopiers. Or radio in all its forms. Or the car. The medium is the message of the technology.

A third approach: Come at teleconferencing from the side instead of head-on. Consider it as a species of TV program, which it is, really. What sort of advertisements might you make for use when there is a suitable pause in the proceedings? That is, what sort of audience have you got to work with and what state is it in? What susceptibilities are available to work with? Disregard the content (the products advertised) or make them innocuous: air travel, for example, or boardroom furniture. This kind of approach will help illuminate the ways in which the technology configures the sensibilities of the users.

Six inches? One or two inches? What sort of intimacy and invasion of personal space does this work-a-day instrument assume as normal? By comparison, how close would you feel comfortable to the same interlocutor, in person. (And how close...if you were blind?) But the telephone likes to isolate the audio sense, in low definition (what do you do when you concentrate? - close your eyes and see). Television likes to bring into play all senses, in low definition, that is, below conscious levels. Videophone failed from a clash of icons. A whole range of new studies needs to be mounted quickly to study the most recent developments: LED screens and laptops, the new HDTV and the rest - all of which will have vastly different properties and effects from those of the older screens. The difference will be on the same order of magnitude as that when black-and-white TV was pushed aside by color TV thirty years ago. Color TV represented a quantum-leap in involvement for the viewer, for color is far more tactile and subliminally involving than gray-scale. (For example, if you see yellow on the screen, it is because the set gave you red and green simultaneously: you mixed them in your eye and you unconsciously made the yellow yourself.)

Teleconferencing as a form pushes job structures, centralism, and hardware to the reversal point. It elevates roles over jobs and changes the nature of power. We used to joke about the businessman who left his home every day and traveled miles downtown to the office to use the telephone. Cellular phones put an end to that. Teleconferencing similarly decentralizes the meeting. It doesn't matter whether you find yourself in Bonn or Boston, in Berne or Brazilia or Brisbane: you can easily be in all of them at once via this new form. It makes possible the crowd-without-walls, the roomless meeting. Like other electric technologies, this one translates the user into electricity itself, and makes the "hardware" fact of the physical body and its limitations and imperfections irrelevant. The resulting new equality bypasses the limitations of the body and imposes a physical and social leveling by simply circumventing human scale and proportion.

The resulting social upheaval, already of enormous scope, has just begun to assert itself. On the telephone, on the air, you exist and operate minus the body, as a disembodied intelligence. You are translated into a condition of pure information: you can be here in Toronto AND here in Sydney at the same time, in two or three or even (via broadcast) a hundred thousand places at once. This metaphysical fact means that the physical bond, which has held us since the dawn of creation, has now been set aside. It has great implications for our senses of identity, personal and corporate. Electronic, discarnate participation is incredibly intimate: only the hardware body – or the intersection of the "hardware" individual body with the "software" intellect – gives a substantial basis for individual, private identity. The "principle of identity" in mathematics is that "things equal to the same thing are equal to each other." In media study there is the correlative principle of identity, that those who participate in the same thing at the same time participate in each other. Partici-pation in video imagery is so profound, and so unconscious, that it overwhelms individual identity even as it robs the private body of its significance. Hence the stupendous power of participational roles and masks mentioned at the outset, and the pressure on the job to engage in team playing instead of specialist job-holding.

For a few years now, the new business of business has been culture, not hardware products. A century ago we could boast that our culture was business-oriented, meaning that politics was an extension of manufacturing and marketing. Given the electrification of the office with computers and the rest, we can now proclaim, "culture is our business." Just consider how much of on-the-job energy is now directed inward, invested in making and maintaining the corporate culture. Group identities are always delicate and precarious, and have to be refurbished from moment to moment. The new competence: Are you a team player? The team shoves aside the old job structure and retrieves the group effort.

It sidesteps the old modes of responsibility for the job and replaces them with new loyalties and conformities: metaphysically, the shift is from becoming to a constant process of being. The independent, the nonconformist, used to command respect; in the new corporate team-culture, the nonconformist is an instant outsider, an alien, to be ostracized. "Not a team player."

A last observation: Teaming has another twist, at least for North Americans. Henry James was one of the first to explore, in his novels, the different habits of use of space of Americans and Europeans. *Daisy Miller*, for one, turned on the fact that when a European goes outside, to a cafe or restaurant or theater, he expects to engage in social life; at home, he expects to find privacy. But North Americans, unlike the rest of the world, which follows the same pattern as Europeans, reverse all this.

North Americans have always gone outside the home for privacy and inside the home for communal life. The North American will unhesitatingly invite complete strangers into the home for dinner or amusement, and the traditional role of the North American housewife was that of hostess. For the same reason, Americans needed large spaces in their homes, and Europeans were quite satisfied with small rooms. (You could know a European for twenty years and never have been invited to his or her home. James Joyce wrote that "an Englishman's home is his coffin.") On the other hand, North Americans expect to find privacy outside the home: on the job, in cafes and theaters, etc. So they have pioneered the drive-in: the drive-in movie theater, bank, restaurant, even drive-in churches and funeral homes.

Every American teenager knows that to find privacy he or she has to go out. Perhaps that is why North American cars were so capacious: they were rooms of ones' own. The last bastion of privacy was the traffic jam, but the cellular telephone has ended that. And the sudden rise of corporate culture and on-the-job teamness has meant the virtual disappearance of privacy at work, leaving the American in considerable straits: Where to find privacy? This constitutes a radical undermining of private identity throughout the culture – a totally unexpected side-effect of the computer and other video technologies, yet consistent with the manner in which they have revolutionized business and work of all kinds. Teleconferencing will add its influence to this pattern.

TO SUM UP:

Every human technology works along four principal axes of development. One: What does it enlarge or enhance or accelerate or extend? Second: What does it retrieve or revive in a more modern or up-to-date form? Third: What does it push aside or make irrelevant or obsolete? Fourth: What formal reversals does it occasion?

Teleconferencing enlarges the cast and the number of sites that can participate in a discussion. It vastly amplifies the nature and character and power of imagery, sidelining the old bottom line of products and policies.

Teleconferencing pushes aside the need to travel to a central location, and so obviates distances and hardware limitations of space, time, national borders and frontiers. It also puts the back-room meeting on stage, retrieving it in its own image, with production values and sets.

Teleconferencing retrieves the distant participant as a disembodied intelligence. It brings back the committee in a new form, one measured in intimate distances, one with theatrical trappings (there has to be a start and stop, a producer, etc.). The tribal council makes its reappearance in showbiz terms, as a production.

Reversals: the specialty network forms part of a global theater in which roles predominate and national borders are irrelevant; national politics yield to overlapping and interpenetrating interests. The user becomes actor/actress. The boardroom becomes center stage. Centralism turns to decentralism, hardware yields to software.

For what new form of business and culture does teleconferencing pave the way? There lies the future of this form. As the technology becomes more sophisticated and we broadcast more and more of ourselves, it leads to another question: Why not dispense with the rest of the bodily and sensory limitations and transmit consciousness itself?

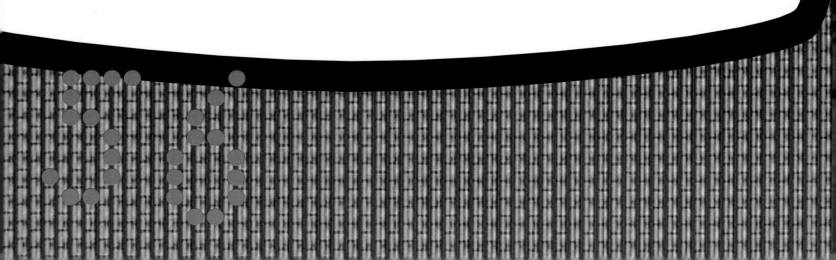

TELECONFERENCING

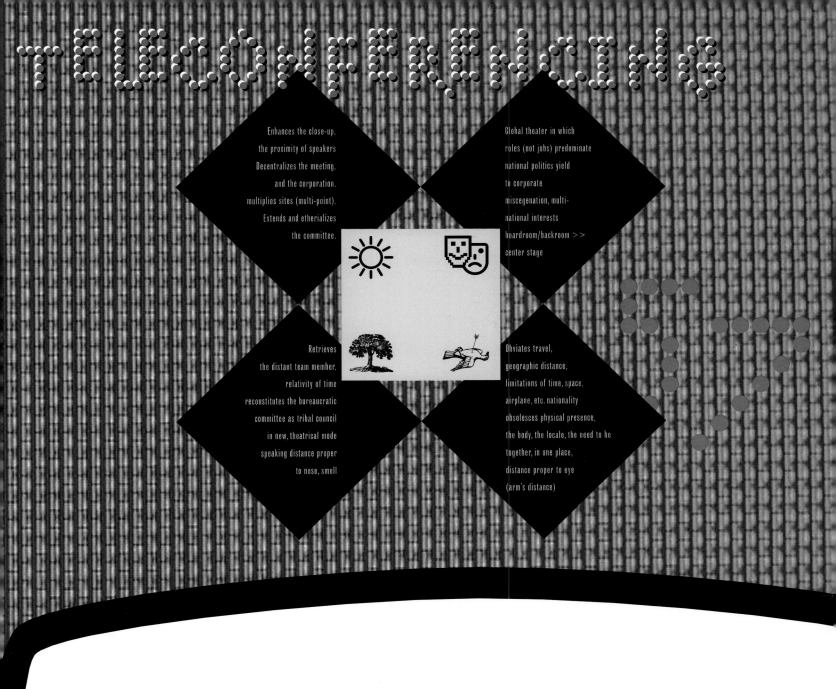

Enhances the close-up,
the proximity of speakers
Decentralizes the meeting,
and the corporation,
multiplies sites (multi-point).
Extends and etherializes
the committee.

Global theater in which
roles (not jobs) predominate
national politics yield
to corporate
miscegenation, multi-
national interests
boardroom/backroom >>
center stage

Retrieves
the distant team member,
relativity of time
reconstitutes the bureaucratic
committee as tribal council
in new, theatrical mode
speaking distance proper
to nose, smell

Obviates travel,
geographic distance,
limitations of time, space,
airplane, etc. nationality
obsolesces physical presence,
the body, the locale, the need to be
together, in one place,
distance proper to eye
(arm's distance)

The ground of effects always paves the way for the causes to arrive, so the "coming events cast their shadows before them." With elevators, airplanes, helicopters, space shuttles, satellites, we have all the effects: anti-gravity will not be long in coming. Radio, telephone, TV, and the rest mean that ESP technology will soon arrive. The only question is who will get to the patent office first.

Lately, while trying to pay some attention to English *sounds*, I realized that it is very difficult to ignore the meanings of words that you know and just listen to the music they make. It's comparatively easy when you don't know the language: just recall the experience you have when you tune in to a radio or TV program in a strange language. All you get then is the music.

For some years now Islamic Arabs have been calling us in North America – speakers of English – the Great Satan. If this is anything more than mindless invective then they must have something definite in mind, but whatever it is eludes us. In general, we think of ourselves as good-hearted, if sometimes bumbling. We wish them nothing but well, on the whole. "The Great Satan" seems to us overstating things somewhat; yet as time passes they grow more, not less, insistent.

Theirs is an ear-world of resonant domes and minarets, of open-air markets all a-buzz; "Koran" means "that which is to be read aloud." They don't *see* sense at all; but they *hear* the English world as certainly Satanic. It's unmistakable – though concealed from us, the English speakers who live immersed in it.

We're the worm in their apple.

We're the snake in their Garden of Eden.

The world 'round, English is called "the hissing language." S is the most conspicuous sound in spoken English. It's also the most frequent initial letter in the alphabet – the OED (Oxford English Dictionary) needs two volumes to handle all of the S-words – but not the most frequent letter. Letter frequency begins e, t, a, o, n, r, i, s, h... Our music – or rather our muzak, because it's environmental and we shun awareness of it – has done us in. Our constant sibilance – the hissing of the great snake.

Culturally, too, we two are antitheses. They are group-people, ear-people, tribal peoples. Our tradition is as eye-folk. We are crowdbane; individualists, private entrepreneurs. All of that merely serves to confirm what their senses have already established pre-consciously. Ssssssssssssshhhhh!

Well, so we hiss, some. What effect has that had on us, enveloped in it? Does it lend sinew or sinuosity to our sensibilities? For ages it has been recognized that the heavy gutturality of German played a part in their never fully detribalizing and in the severity with which they were assaulted by the medium of radio.

What does it do to you when your characteristic sound, your unconscious keynote, is formed forward in the mouth, not back, back down in the throat? Does it make it easier for your culture to be outgoing? Forward? Entrepreneurial?

A language is not a medium

for messages but an organ of perception, collective, corporate perception.

The discovery that

languages are not

channels like the telegraph

or little messages
but basically

forms of perception

and association by perception

has been

a tremendous revolution in literature.

—*Marshall McLuhan,*
"The Meaning of TV
to Children"

Why has no one ever commented on the strange media bias that stirs the discord between the Croats and the Serbs in the former Yugoslavia? And why haven't we seen any discussion of how that bias profoundly controls the political alliances that surround the conflict?

Here, surely, is one of the epic demonstrations of our time of the power of sheer media not to mediate but to disrupt relations between peoples. Here is a demonstration,

An Ancient Quarrel in Modern Europe – and the Enduring Mystery of English

if ever there was one, of the power of media themselves to implant powerful unconscious bias in their users. Every technology of communication instills an unconscious bias in the sensory lives of the users, a new configuration of perception that brings with it a freshly heightened sensitivity to self and society. Electric media in particular arouse and exaggerate the most ancient and deeply rooted tribal loyalties and antipathies. Violence is the only means of preserving or reestablishing an identity under such extreme circumstances.

These two groups, Croat and Serb, read and write exactly the same language – Serbo-Croatian –

but use subtly different writing systems.

What they write about, the content, can be disregarded as a factor because it is largely the same. They read, for example, exactly the same news and advertisements in their newspapers. But the one group reads and writes in the Greco-Roman alphabet, the same alphabet that we use; the other, in the Cyrillic alphabet, which is used to write Russian, Bulgarian, and so on.

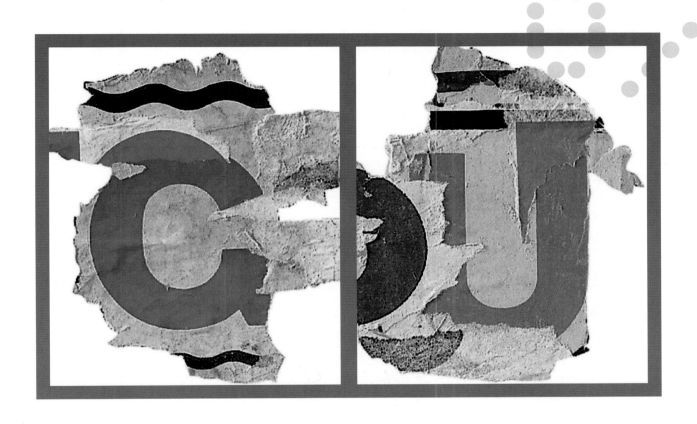

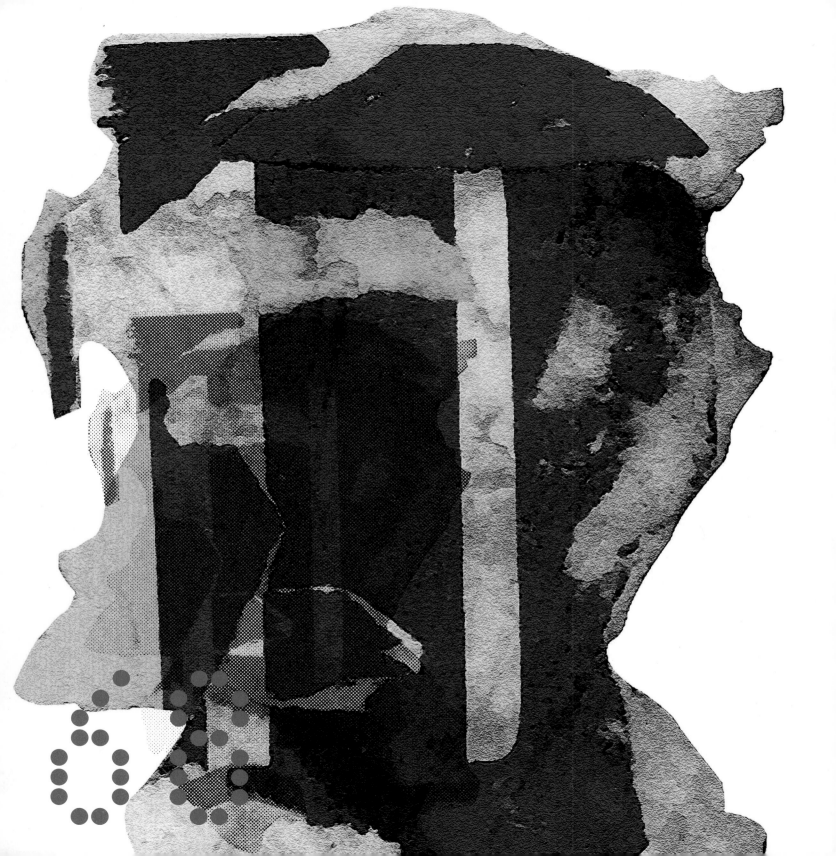

It is no simple coincidence,

then, that the United States places its military backing behind the group that uses its very alphabet and that the Russians put theirs behind the group that writes with their Cyrillic system. But consider: Is any other alignment conceivable? We simply could NOT by any stretch even imagine ourselves backing Cyrillic-writers against users of our own alphabet, any more than we could imagine the Russians backing

our alphabet against their own.

Our unconscious bias is far too strong to allow us to do otherwise than we do.

At this point, it is worth recalling Winston Churchill's observation that the second world war – the radio war – pitted English against the other languages: German, Japanese, Italian, etc. That is, English lined up Britain, the United States, Canada, Australia, and so on. (Ireland is conspicuously missing, but was at the time undergoing her own massive tribal retrieval of selfhood and the Celtic language.) And it is also curious that the main protagonists in the battle were the two main branches of the Teutonic language, English and German, which are closer than mortal cousins. There is much truth to the old saw that similarity is the soul of competition – and competition is warfare in low definition.

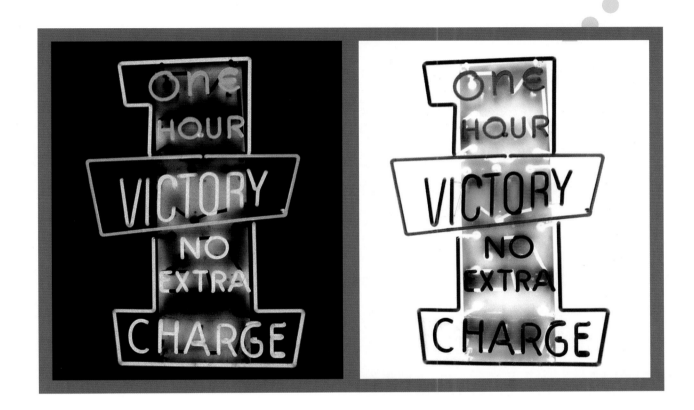

Evidently there is something about English itself that instills in its users a resilience or resistance to electricity.

That defers or deflects or delays its depredations.

That creates areas of insensitivity, of numbness. That insulates us from its effects. (Germany, resistless, tumbled headlong into the tribal trap.) We might well meditate on what that mysterious quality might be, for mystery it is. Everyone about us, it seems, is going on the tribal trip of group identity. North America's native Indians, Canada's French, America's blacks, the Spanish, even many of our women, and our children (until they grow up some)

all are sucker-punc. the electron

ed by

Yet English-speaking men remain comparatively phlegmatic.

Is there some inherent remedy in simply being of Anglo-Saxon stock? Is it necessary to BE Anglo-Saxoned by birth or can one "get" it by assimilating the language – and pretty much forsaking one's own (like Czech or Basque or Erse)? Apparently, English serves as the folk remedy that inoculates against some of the ills of electronic culture.

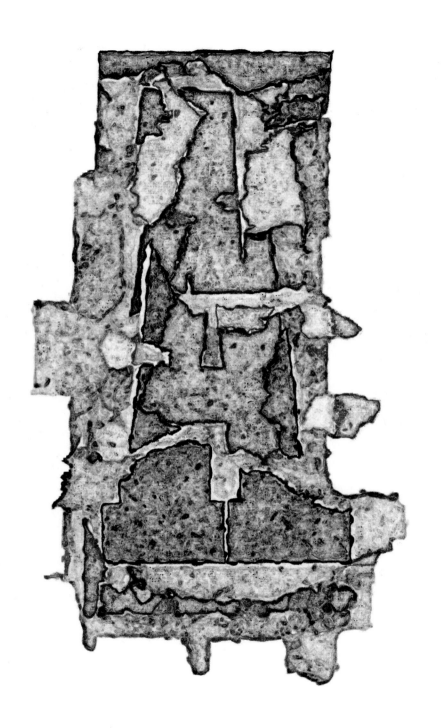

>Does English Dominate the Internet?

(Reuters)

At the Francophonie summit in West Africa, French President Jacques Chirac contended that the info-highway imperils the French language and culture. Canadian Prime Minister Jean Chretien countered that the French language

"must make its own way or be left by the wayside." – *The Globe and Mail*, 4 December 1995

Note that the number one Internet language is English. Number two is Spanish.

In articles about the effects of technology, you frequently see the charge of "technological determinism" leveled at the approach to media study used by Marshall McLuhan and others. Those who use the term mean by it a sleight-of-hand trickery with cause and effect: they suspect a sort of large-scale covert behaviorism. They are uneasy because McLuhan's approach to media exposes interrelations and patterns that their own "proper" approaches do not reveal to them.

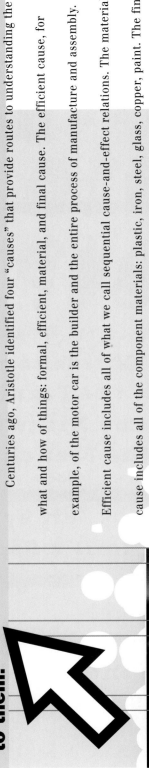

Centuries ago, Aristotle identified four "causes" that provide routes to understanding the what and how of things: formal, efficient, material, and final cause. The efficient cause, for example, of the motor car is the builder and the entire process of manufacture and assembly.

Efficient cause includes all of what we call sequential cause-and-effect relations. The material cause includes all of the component materials: plastic, iron, steel, glass, copper, paint. The final cause is the final product, the car as a thing in itself, the *figure* apart from its *ground*. But the formal cause has always been a mystery to alphabetic Westerners, because it is the *ground*. For the car, the formal cause is the entire situation: the user, the highway, and all of the side-effects that the car occasions.

Most of what our culture usually calls "media study" involves the first three causes. Concern over the effects of violence on television, for example, stems from the suspicion that there is a direct, efficient-cause (cause-and-effect) connection between the portrayal and the incidence of violence in children and in society. (One observer remarked that there is also a great deal of comedy on television, but we don't see people committing comedy at home or in the streets as a result.) Think about it: were such connections real, for example, advertisers would long ago have taken complete charge of free will. But still, efficient cause (combined with material and final) remains the favored theory of communication of the literati: it is the only connected, rational mode of causality. Determinism involves connection.

Blind Spots, and the Rear-view Mirror

Clearly, the reproach "technological determinism!" does not apply to media study of the other variety, that practiced by Harold Innis, Marshall McLuhan, Eric Havelock, Lynn White Jr., *et al.* (To the contrary, McLuhan maintained this constant theme in his writing and public lectures: "there is absolutely no inevitability as long as there is a willingness to contemplate what is happening" [*The Medium Is the Massage*, 1967, p. 25].) These people work with formal cause, not efficient cause; with pattern, ground, and sensibility. The *ground* is the formal cause of the *figure*, in every case and in every sense. The audience is the formal cause of the ad; the reader, the formal cause of the poem; the listener, the formal cause of the music. All of our media are active forms and have to be studied formally in order to understand their power to transform.

But "technological determinism!" does appear, interestingly, to be the stock response of many sociologists and "communications specialists" when they come face to face with formal causality. It signals their inability to think in any terms except those of connection and efficient cause. That failing, evidently, characterizes their general philosophical approach to the world.

"Technological determinism!" can, however, apply to the routine kinds of philosophical and sociological "media study" – descriptive, content approaches – because they are based on efficient cause (the reigning mode of science). It also applies very well to a great deal of what is called Futurology, when that is stripped of its hucksterism for novelty and its disdain for the present and the past.

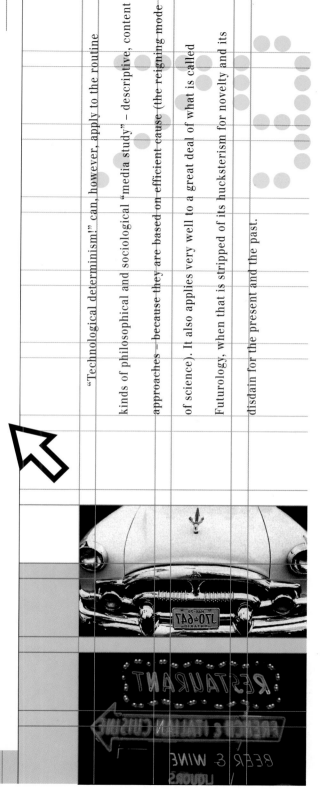

Blind Spots, and the Rear-view Mirror

It may also be that "technological determinism" actually identifies a fallacy of the post hoc ergo propter hoc ("after, therefore because of this") variety: if so, it stands for a valid qualm. Even a brief acquaintance with *ground* reveals a galaxy of unexpected and irrational connections: a normal reaction to this sudden awareness takes one of two forms, paranoia or denial ("determinism").

But to apply the term to McLuhan *et al.*, however, one must have missed their point rather completely.

Francis Bacon suggested that there were four main kinds of ignorance, four fundamental blind spots concerning media, culture, and society. He called them Idols, false gods that divert attention and devotion and distract from truth and wisdom. (See his *New Science*; the *Novum Organum, or True Directions Concerning the Interpretation of Nature*, Book I, axioms xli-xliv.) His famous statement about the distortions of our sense of things due to intellectual and perceptual bias echoes thousands of years of traditional observation: *For the mind of man is far from the nature of a clear and equal glass [mirror] wherein the beams of things should reflect according to their true incidence; nay, it is rather like an enchanted glass, full of superstition and imposture, if it be not delivered and reduced (The Advancement of Learning).*

The first kind of false god, the Idols of the Tribe, identifies the bias that prevents us from seeing things in their own right. These environmental distortions of perception derive from our human tendency to ignore our assumptions or from our self-imposed media – man-made environments.

Bacon gives this: The Idols of the Tribe have their foundation in human nature itself, and in the tribe or race of men. For it is a false assertion that the sense of man is the measure of things. On the contrary, all perceptions as well of the senses as of the mind, are according to the measure of the individual and not according to the measure of the universe. And the human understanding is like a false mirror, which, receiving rays irregularly, distorts and discolors the nature of things by mingling its own nature with it.

The second kind he called the Idols of the Cave, to pinpoint how intellectual laziness and dogmatism result in distortion and ignorance. (The "Cave" in question is the famous cave of Plato in *The Republic*, Book VII.) The Idols of the Cave are the idols of the individual man. For everyone (besides the errors common to human nature in general) has a cave or den of his own, which refracts and discolors the light of nature; owing either to his own proper and peculiar nature or to his education and conversation with others; or to the reading of books and the authority of those whom he esteems and admires…or the like.

A third kind of stupidity Bacon called the Idols of the Marketplace. These have their roots in language and terminology, and in social and cultural preferences. There are also idols formed by the intercourse and association of men with each other, which I call Idols of the Market-place, on account of the commerce and consort of men there. For it is by discourse that men associate; and words are imposed according to the apprehension of the vulgar. And therefore the ill and unfair choice of words wonderfully obstructs the understanding. Nor do the definitions or explanations wherewith in some things learned men are wont to guard and defend themselves, by any means set the matter right. But words plainly force and overrule the understanding, and throw all into confusion, and lead men away into numberless empty controversies and idle fancies.

Finally, there are the Idols of the Theater, which cover intellectual arrogance, the tendency of narrow specialism (in theory and science) to insist on its universality.

Lastly, there are the idols which have immigrated into men's minds from the various dogmas of philosophies, and also from wrong laws of demonstration. These I call Idols of the Theater; because in my judgment all the received systems are but so many stage-plays, representing worlds of their own creation after an unreal and scenic fashion....Neither again do I mean this only of entire systems, but also of many principles and axioms in science, which by tradition, credulity, and negligence have come to be received.

It is this last kind of bias, that conferred by specialism, that blinds experts to seeing media as forms and as constituting new *grounds* for culture and society alike. The misunderstanding that results from the specialist approach to non-specialist *ground* and media leads directly to the charge, "Determinism!"

How many ways do you suppose the four kinds of idolatry pervade our present world in various new disguises? Which, for example, appears most often in advertising? In politics? In the academy? In business? In entertainment? (I leave to you, reader, the fun of discovering how Aristotle's causes relate to Bacon's Idols.)

A detective story sets out to re-create an action that is perceived as flawed or breached. It is the missing link or gap in the sequence of events that inspires the participation of the reader in completing the pattern of events. The job of the novelist like that of the criminal is to dazzle and distract the eye of the unwary with *figures*, to play with and manipulate the blind spots; the job of the detective, to discern the truth in the *ground*-pattern of influence and circumstance. The detective has to work from formal cause (the situation) to the perpetrator (efficient cause); so the detective begins with the effect and works backwards. The artist works in a similar manner to reveal the present, which is always invisible to ordinary attention.

One characteristic of all social processes is that they become manifest and conspicuous, for the first time, at the moment of their demise – as what was once *ground* becomes *figure.*

Art has predictive power precisely because it works from the present *ground* and by means of percepts (the senses) rather than concepts (ideas).

So art serves as the rear-view mirror on the car or chariot of culture.

The rear-view mirror is not an instrument for taking a nostalgia trip. Any car or truck driver, facing front, sees the straight-ahead panorama quite clearly but has specific blind spots. No one spends his or her time driving the family car while gazing longingly or sentimentally in the rear-view mirror – without promptly inducing a crash. The mirror is there as a safeguard, to keep the driver aware of what is happening *in the blind spots*. So, to say for example that "the medium is the rear-view mirror" is to miss the meaning of both.

The rear-view mirror provides a means of clairvoyance in the darkness imposed by a medium (which Bacon called an Idol). Like serious art, it turns the hidden cultural *ground* into *figure*. It has nothing to do with the past, and everything to do with the present – the pressant, the press of events steaming up on you in your blind spot and about to overtake you and roll over you.

The rear-view mirror is a device for forecasting the present.

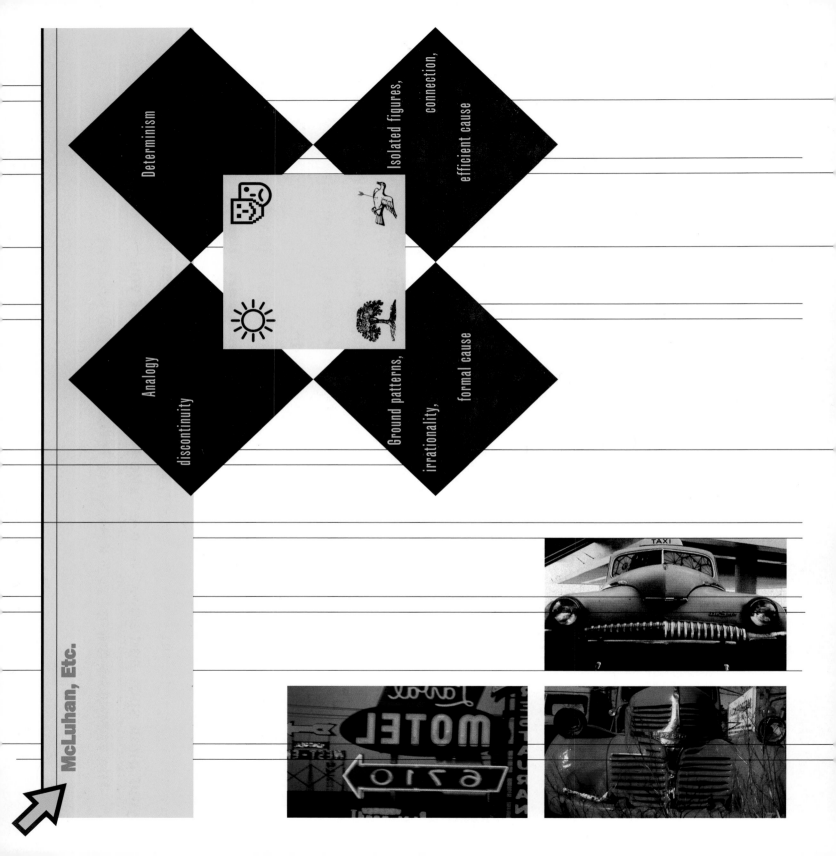

Determinism

Isolated figures,
connection,
efficient cause

Analogy

discontinuity

Ground patterns,
irrationality,

formal cause

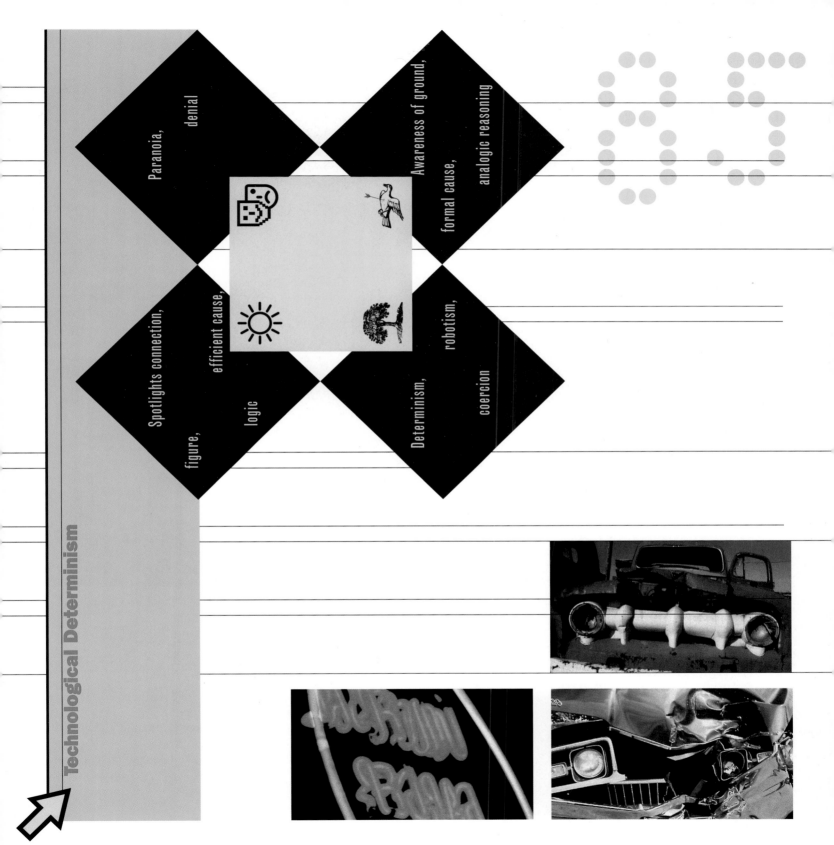

Technological Determinism

Paranoia, denial

Awareness of ground, formal cause, analogic reasoning

Spotlights connection, efficient cause, figure, logic

Determinism, robotism, coercion

Postliteracy

[The gist of an address to the Ontario Council of Teachers of English, 1988; a version of this essay appeared in the journal *indirections*, vol. 13, no. 1, June 1989, published by the OCTE.]

The hi-tech book does not exist. Anything "read" off a TV or computer screen has the form of TV or computer and produces (as best it can) the satisfactions of TV or the computer. *Sesame Street* has not produced a generation of Matthew Arnolds or Samuel Johnsons. Nor could it. And neither will the word-processor – another mode of television. Like all other media, the alphabet is a drug: it is addictive, as TV is addictive or the telephone is addictive, or the car is addictive.

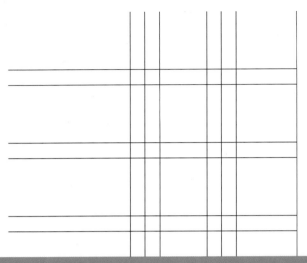

On every hand we see evidence that our culture is thoroughly immersed in postliteracy. How many of the people around us do not aspire to greater literacy or powers of discrimination? How many find literacy too slow or unrewarding? How many, given leisure, could read but prefer some other entertainment? The "coffee-table book" is one element of our postliterate milieu. This is not to indict such books but to notice that a literate society has little or no use for them. They are not serious literature, and they don't pretend to be. They offer few rewards to a literate sensibility. They are not intended to be

In all of human history only four ways to write have been invented: alphabet, syllabary, ideogram, and pictogram.

The phonetic alphabet is the most extreme, the most abstract form of writing. Alphabets, such as the Greek, Cyrillic, or Roman, have comparatively few characters (between twenty and forty). Each character is inherently meaningless. It stands for a sound that also is inherently meaningless.

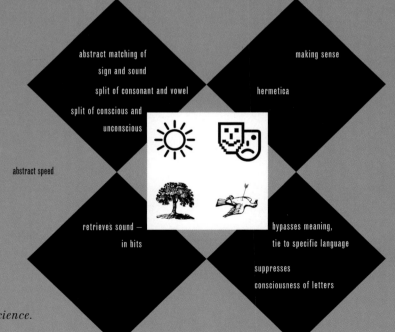

abstract matching of
sign and sound

making sense

split of consonant and vowel

hermetica

split of conscious and
unconscious

abstract speed

retrieves sound —
in bits

bypasses meaning,
tie to specific language

suppresses
consciousness of letters

Note: For a fuller discussion, see Eric Havelock,

Preface to Plato, and *The Origins of Greek Literacy*;

McLuhan and McLuhan, *Laws of Media: The New Science.*

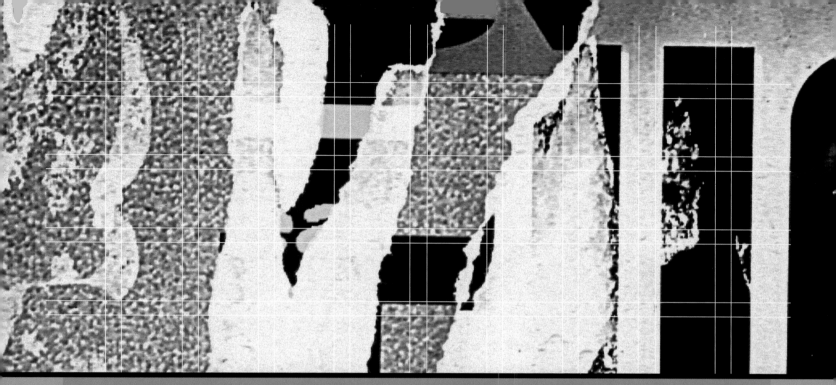

Syllabaries account for most of the writing systems ever invented.

Syllabaries tend to have a large number of characters, often over two hundred, but sometimes as few as seventy or eighty. Each character of a syllabary stands for an entire syllable, a "whole sound," so "Sesame" (as in *Sesame Street*) would take three characters: se + sa + me. Because each syllabary character carries a lot of information, it takes relatively few to spell words; whereas each character of a phonetic alphabet carries relatively little information so it takes proportionately more to spell words.

represents whole sounds
(consonant plus vowels)

babble, stutter

retrieves meaning —
in bits

flow of speech

scrutinized or studied; they are supposed to be looked at and enjoyed as aesthetic objects. They are the book-as-furniture.

The phonetic alphabet produced Aristotle and Euclid and developed in us what Aristotle termed the rational mind, which we now call the left hemisphere of the brain. Plato took aim at the right hemisphere – the mimetic and poetic faculty. It is crucial that we know the alphabet and its effects if we want to understand its vulnerabilities and relation to our present condition. Like other media, the alphabet translated experience from one form into another, replaced one kind of sensibility with another.

The alphabet translates the multi-sensory experience of the resonant, uttered word into experience for one sense alone: the eye. Eric Havelock has

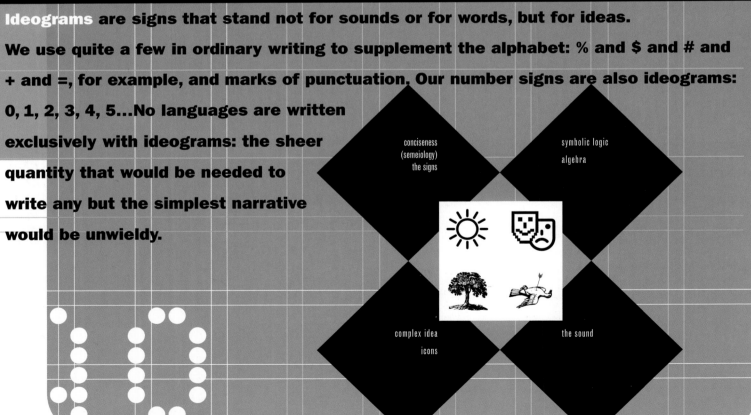

Ideograms are signs that stand not for sounds or for words, but for ideas. We use quite a few in ordinary writing to supplement the alphabet: % and $ and # and + and =, for example, and marks of punctuation. Our number signs are also ideograms: 0, 1, 2, 3, 4, 5...No languages are written exclusively with ideograms: the sheer quantity that would be needed to write any but the simplest narrative would be unwieldy.

conciseness
(semeiology)
the signs

symbolic logic
algebra

complex idea
icons

the sound

detailed how the alphabet gets its power from the discovery of the consonant –

a complete figment of the imagination. And this must be THE central mystery

of Western civilization: whatever possessed its inventors even to imagine the

consonant, and to invent the alphabet of phonemes?

The phonetic consonant doesn't exist alone: it is always accompanied by

a vowel which it shapes or determines. People don't experience consonants as

separate things, but they do experience syllables. So the syllabary is a reason-

able invention. Our alphabetic letters are inherently meaningless; the sounds

they re-present are meaningless, too: that makes two levels of abstraction.

Furthermore, in reading, a deep divorce is introduced between conscious and

subconscious: that is, some things are supposed to be ignored (for example,

Only the Chinese and Japanese write using pictograms – writing with pictures:

the Chinese lexicon contains some 40,000 characters.

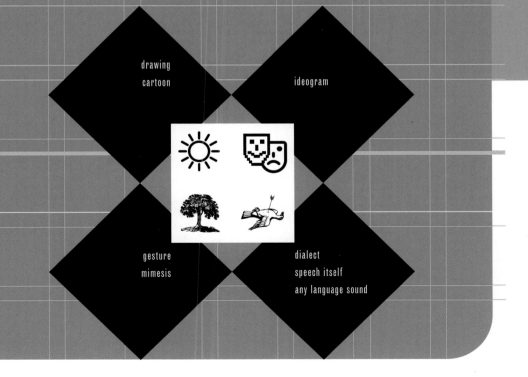

drawing
cartoon

ideogram

gesture
mimesis

dialect
speech itself
any language sound

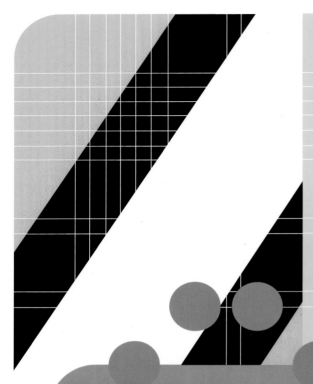

the individual letters, the page itself). The alphabet gives us the first example of an institutionalized subconscious.

As the senses split apart, as sound separates from eye, knower from known, conscious from unconscious, the individual puts on this new power of fragmentation and separates from the group, pulls the private consciousness away from the collective unconsciousness. Immediately is born the *civis*, the private individual, the root of *civi*lization. (Technically, then, cultures that have not developed individualism cannot be called civilized, however refined or sophisticated they may have become.) Plato attacked the poets on quite reasonable grounds: preliterate poetics entirely circumvents and subverts the private awareness that was just emerging in his time and of which he was the

Curiously, the four ways to write also relate to each other in proper proportion, as follows:

alphabet is to ideogram

specialized awareness **as** **inclusive awareness**

syllabary is to pictogram

herald and champion. You can't *be* the thing *and* know it abstractly at the same time.

The alphabet's extreme power of abstracting and splitting lets the user write any language, by ignoring meanings and focusing only on the sound system. No other writing system – syllabary, pictogram, ideogram – has this power of abstract mobility. Anything that attacks these properties of the alphabet simultaneously cuts at the root of literacy. "Hypocrite lecteur," wrote Baudelaire: "mask-wearing reader": the end of objectivity: the reader puts on the poem and becomes the poet's accomplice. Immersion kills objectivity.

Reading aloud ended with the telegraph. The "trilling wire" of the new nerve system outside the body private and social drove readers to explore the inner landscape and to drop delivery to the outer audience. Silent reading became the norm everywhere. Reading speeds promptly doubled or tripled, and the inner voice, silent for centuries (the one Julian Jaynes reported in *The Origin of Consciousness in the Breakdown of the Bicameral Mind*), took over narration. The telegraph office was the box-office entrance to the movie theater of the mind.

The familiar "mental movie" we experience when reading a novel is really only available to the high-speed (silent) passive reader. With delivery aloud, the reader faces the audience; when silent, inner and outer coalesce. Film and stream-of-consciousness style were inevitable, both embedded in telegraph form. In the same way, all electric media push us inwards and dissolve the alphabetic split of inner/outer and of conscious/subconscious by turning every experience into fantasy. All turns inner. Tribal voices.

In *The Alphabetization of the Popular Mind*, Ivan Illich points out that

Huckleberry Finn was one of the first books intended to be read silently. To read it aloud, then, is to falsify it as much as to read Jonson or Shakespeare or Goldsmith silently, as if they were modern novels, is to falsify them. The aesthetics are entirely different. Should not any trained, sensitive reader be able to tell immediately from the experience the text provides which books were written in the new style – for silent treatment? This sheds light on why T. S. Eliot reckoned Mark Twain on a par with Dryden and Swift.

Eliot wrote, consciously, for the electrified. By his time, electrocution had replaced elocution as a mode of sensibility: "The Waste Land" is a footnote to that condition. His essay, "Tradition and the Individual Talent," aimed to bring our awareness of literature up to date, to attune it to the new right-brain sensibility. He lagged Ezra Pound's "The Serious Artist" by a few years and Newman's *Essay on Development* by a few decades. Eliot's essay is far more revolutionary than Einstein's papers on the General and Special Theories of Relativity, for example, because he was much more conscious of what he was doing. Eliot rendered the greater service: Einstein exploited the new sensibility; Eliot explored and dissected it. And Eliot's work can be applied to Einstein, but not vice-versa.

Is it simple good fortune that no one, no Department of Literature, has realized that Eliot's essay might be taken seriously enough to be used? Three-quarters of a century after it was written, it is still far ahead of the literati. He wrote that what we call tradition comprises a *simultaneous* whole that transforms the meaning of any individual artist – and vice-versa: any individual artist has the same reciprocal effect on the entire tradition. "The tradition," then, is not as we have been taught a simple sequence or parade of

writers with great reputations but a simultaneous order in which Homer has as much effect on Cervantes or Flaubert or Allan Ginsberg or W. P. Kinsella as they have on Homer. Eliot's revolutionary – and now obvious – idea was that the past writers could be changed by the present influence. So the past influences the present, well enough; and to exactly the same degree the present influences the past. Imagine the revolution if one taught literature along those lines.

Einstein just transformed some of physics. Eliot presented the means to revolutionize all of the arts, sciences, culture, history.

The same interior robot that reads our novels to us is currently programmed by a broad spectrum of, well, not exactly well-wishers. Begin with "muzak." Include pop music, mass advertising... With muzak, at the peak of form of Western culture, as it were, we have sired a mode of music designed

356

expressly to be ignored. And, when ignored, to have a specific effect. Deliberate, *programmed* ignorance, like all "programming." When you pay attention to it, it stops working.

Anything constantly repeated has the same environmental effect: it becomes an object of *in*attention. Just when attention drops to zero its power reaches its peak as a new program for the subconscious that turns the user into a robot. It simply bypasses the intellect and the conscious faculties, rendering them obsolescent. We retain only the dream of autonomy we used to take for granted. So much for the "rational soul" and alphabetic man – and the illusion of detachment in our time. The only possible strategy, then, for recovering control is too distasteful and too arduous for the average person. If you pay attention to the ad or the muzak, if you study it and render it conscious, it can't work. The reason most ads present so little to occupy the rational faculties is that they are not for the rational faculties. Non-rational knowledge is mimetic and instantaneous, and instantly satisfying. Reading is too slow. These forms are to be worn, not thought about. They are for participating in.

The more that is recorded about you in the data banks, the more you cease to exist. You are translated into software and imagery, infinitely malleable. The medium is the massage. What conceivable use is privacy to the postliterate? Minus a private identity such as only the phonetic alphabet affords, privacy is meaningless. In fact, such an abstract way to think of one's relation to others in a participational society is not just passé but counter-cultural. The residue is solitude – the biggest social disease of our time.

The average person today has, by and large, no firm sense of the paragraph or of larger organization. Grammar, for most, is a residue of supersti-

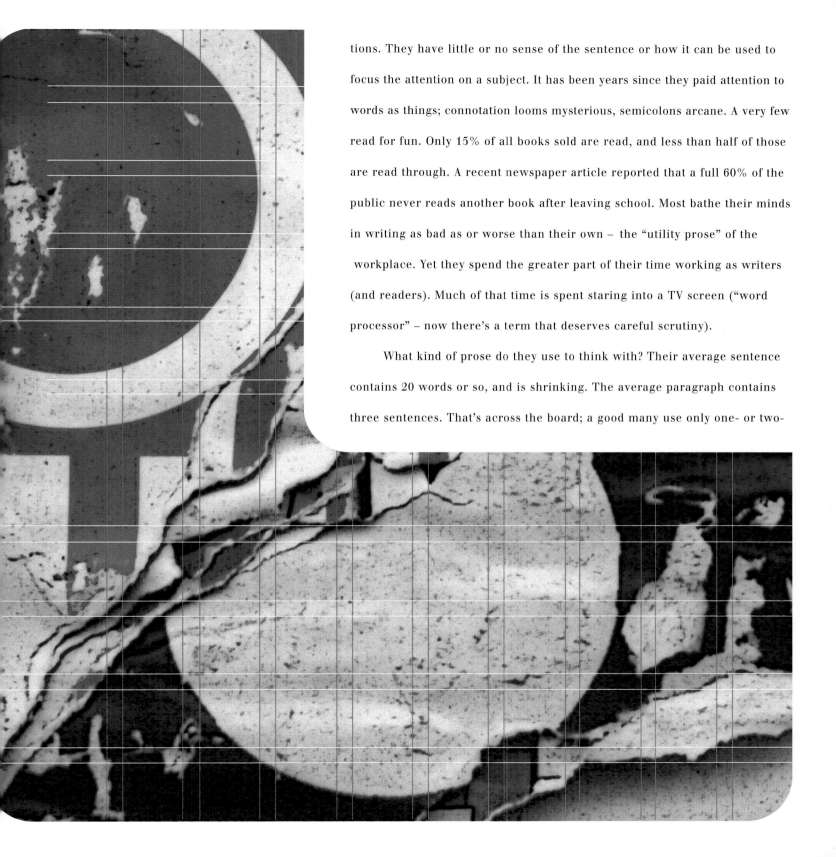

tions. They have little or no sense of the sentence or how it can be used to focus the attention on a subject. It has been years since they paid attention to words as things; connotation looms mysterious, semicolons arcane. A very few read for fun. Only 15% of all books sold are read, and less than half of those are read through. A recent newspaper article reported that a full 60% of the public never reads another book after leaving school. Most bathe their minds in writing as bad as or worse than their own – the "utility prose" of the workplace. Yet they spend the greater part of their time working as writers (and readers). Much of that time is spent staring into a TV screen ("word processor" – now there's a term that deserves careful scrutiny).

What kind of prose do they use to think with? Their average sentence contains 20 words or so, and is shrinking. The average paragraph contains three sentences. That's across the board; a good many use only one- or two-sentence paragraphs. Consider: a one-sentence paragraph is, in normal literate prose, used either for dramatic effect or for transition. Two- or three-sentence groups cannot function as paragraphs: they simply do not yield adequate room for a topic sentence and rational development and transition. This current kind of prose is highly kinetic and dramatic. It achieves a feeling of momentum and urgency, even of impatience.

Brief sentences and small sentence-groups are natural to people with a short attention-span: prose, as always, is tailored to fit the mind of the reader. Compound and compound-complex sentences are scarcely to be found; semi-colon use is rare, and hesitant. Therefore, complex sentences and simple ones abound. Furthermore, a brand-new style has emerged from these conditions, one suited to the new sensibility and one not taught in the curriculum: point-form writing. Point-form is, as it were, pointillist prose for the workplace. It bears no relation to paragraph-style, linear prose or rational organization. Neither is it a form of list-building. That is, it doesn't derive from either of those earlier forms. Point-form presents a set of vignettes, of caricatures and highlights only. At best, it is highly compressed statement. It leans towards aphorism. It surfaced first, perhaps, in executive summaries; now it appears more and more frequently in reports, letters, memos. It features the snapshot statement and graphic layout, not chains of ideas. The training-ground for writing this style, ideally, should be verse, not prose. This is writing for (and by) the right side of the brain. Hello, Heraclitus!

Postliteracy isn't so much the end of literacy as the onset of phase IV: it follows deciphering, manuscript culture, and the intense print phase that peaked between the sixteenth and nineteenth centuries. We are now well over

the dividing line that was the 1960s and '70s.

Postliteracy will bring with it a renaissance of literacy – but in renaissances the old thing always returns in a new form. Probably the most exquisite or most mannered writing is yet to come, something with the trembling delicacy of oriental dance or calligraphy.

Quite likely we will see literary skills reorganized and stratified. One part of the spectrum might feature literacy as simply utilitarian, without particular refinement, like bachelor cooking. Indeed, much "utility prose" is already at this ebb: read a few technical manuals or reports. No one reads – or writes – them for enjoyment or amusement. A second level would find writing as a polite accomplishment, on a par with needlepoint or playing the violin – for private aesthetic satisfaction. A third level contains a relatively small group comparable perhaps to our classical musicians, able to perform across the entire spectrum of literacy, versed in the Western tradition – an elite or aristocracy. They alone will have access to full rational powers of abstraction and detachment, will be able to engage or suppress the voice of the inner robot. They will be in enormous demand because of their critical, logical, and innovative skills, their ability to tap the left brain and suppress the right. They will probably not be the leaders – unless one or another turns pirate or entrepreneur.

These three stages do not comprise a continuous spectrum, just phases of activity. The middle one – historically the largest part – is even now fading rapidly. What use is the literate guy in a postliterate society? Bruce Powe called him *The Solitary Outlaw*. Hired gun? Satirist? Slave?

How can we respond to postliteracy?

The usual response today: redefine literacy so that the "problem" evaporates. Call it "information handling" or "word processing" or something similar. This is the "drowning technique": books are just one of a range of "information options." This ploy is already widely used to deflect concern and divert attention.

Or, change the ground rules. If the alphabet is obsolescent as a writing system, bring in one of the other forms. Perhaps one of them can be brought into tune with the kind of sensibility that prevails. Admit it: the phonetic alphabet is exclusively left-brain in all of its properties. Too severe. Instead, why not explore using a writing system with some (or lots of) right-brain properties rather than sticking with the old alphabet? If the alphabet has served its turn, why not ditch it and replace it with its closest cousin, a syllabary? At least we could save literacy and our literary tradition for a few generations more.

THREE NEW STYLES:
THE POETICS OF THE PC

Three New Styles: The Poetics of the PC

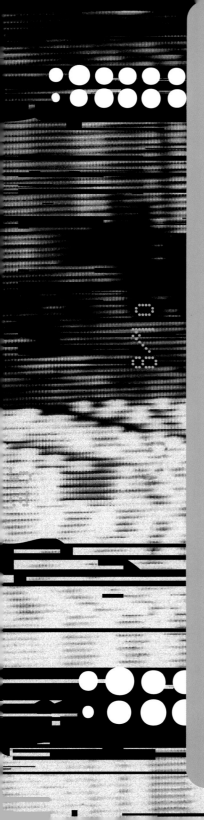

Fully nine-tenths of the writing done today takes place inside businesses, hidden from public awareness. The conspicuous part, in books, newspapers, and periodicals, is slight by comparison.

Today, nearly all prose writing in North America is being done on desktop computers. During the last fifteen years, that computer screen has wrought a number of changes in writing styles which taken together constitute a revolution. These changes result from the way in which the screen reshapes the attention of the users. It works through the right hemisphere of the brain, not just because of the light-through character and the mosaic image, but also because of the near-instantaneous speed: all three combine to generate intense involvement. (See also pp. 46-48 and 187.)

Using the emotionally involving right hemisphere instead of the linear and abstract left side has resulted in shorter attention spans. On average, sentences today are measurably briefer than they were fifteen or twenty years ago. More, the shape and nature of the paragraph has changed utterly.

A paragraph used to be defined as made of, on average, seven to ten sentences that deal with a common subject. One of the sentences announced the topic, and paragraph coherence was enhanced by using transitions and logical connectives between sentences. Additional transitions joined the paragraph to others before and after it. That held until about twenty years ago.

Seven to ten sentences? It has been a long time since business or journalistic prose used the like. Such writing moves far too slowly: it is not compatible with the speed of modern life. It is conspicuously absent from advertising, which sticks to the fiction that it presents rational argument and promotes making "choices."

Average sentence length can be taken as one measure of a reader's attention span. If sentence length in a piece of writing is on the average too long, it overtaxes the reader, and few readers will endure it for long (without literary training or compelling inducement). The reader simply puts down the book or turns to another article.

Paragraph length, another measure of attention span, is a more subtle matter. Still, as recently as a century ago, popular writers reveled in being able to construct clear and enjoyable paragraphs two to three pages long (600 to 1,000 words) and more, and readers willingly read them. Now, no one would dare subject readers to two-page paragraphs, not even in the driest academic or bureaucratic writing. Even the legal profession, notorious for its tedious prose, is in the throes of a "plain language" movement. Today, two-page paragraphs are written deliberately to *discourage* readership, to help the writer conceal matters that must be stated but not noticed.

We readers have lost the taste, and the capacity, for long sequences of words and chains of reasoning. The schools are not to blame here: they haven't yet noticed what is going on. And no one sold us the idea that the old styles were too demanding: no theory is to blame. The new styles arrived as a direct effect of our switching from left to right hemisphere in our imaginative and sensory lives, a shift brought about by long immersing our minds in a milieu composed of TV and computer screens. We have simply undergone a profound change in taste. The result for prose style has been a noticeable decline in sentence and paragraph length and structure.

Average sentences thirty or forty years ago were still, on average, twenty-five or so words long. Today, they are nudging eighteen words in most writing, and have dropped to as little as six or eight words in the "Harlequin Romance" genre. (I take these numbers from counting average sentence length in best-selling books from the immediate postwar era to the present.)

Paragraphs have undergone a much more drastic revolution. It is no exaggeration to say that writing with "word-processors" has seen three distinct new styles emerge as the average workaday paragraph shrank from seven sentences to six, to five, four, three, two, one, and, now, even less. By and large, now, the ten-sentence paragraph is a thing of the past. Most business and public writing – and that means most writing – now uses a staccato style of one-sentence paragraphs, or a more fluid running style of two- and three-sentence paragraphs, or the new-minted style called point-form (or bullet form).

The rhetorical dimensions of these three "new" styles tell much about their users.

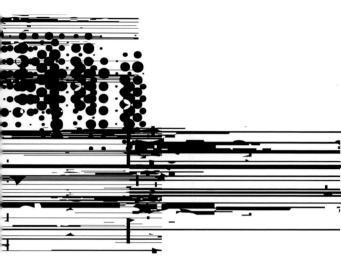

One-sentence Paragraphs: Staccato Style

Sentences and paragraphs were designed to do different jobs. What happens when they merge?

A sentence should embody a complete thought or idea.

Each new idea demands a separate sentence.

Formerly, a complicated idea called for a long sentence, one that might have taken ten or fifteen lines. In our time, as attention spans declined, so did sentence length. Consequently, that same complex idea will now be parceled into four or five sentences.

A similar fate befell the paragraph, which was designed to contain or dispose of a complete topic. One sentence (usually the first or the last) would announce the topic and the others would support or elaborate on it in depth. But paragraphs, too, relate to attention span and have now shrunk to two or three sentences, or to one. The result: a new style.

Huge tire blaze doused --at last

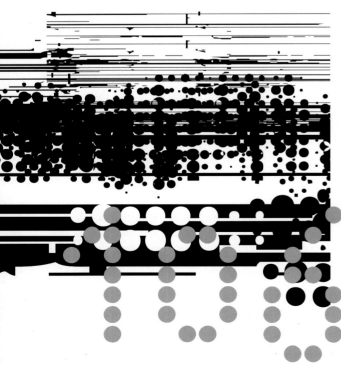

By Leslie Papp
TORONTO STAR

HAGERSVILLE — After 17 days of stubborn resistance, the Great Tire Fire here is vanquished.

"We've won," Jim Coulson of the Ontario Fire Marshal's office said yesterday, a wide grin splitting his face.

The 40-member crew is riding an emotional high, said Bob Thomas, spokesman for Ontario's natural resources ministry.

"They know they've done something nobody else has done before," he said.

Firefighters at the scene were jubilant, posing amid the muck, in their smoke-stained yellow coats, for a group photo.

"Everyone's feeling pretty good," said firefighter John Hadley of Cornwall, who can't wait for "a hot shower."

The men joked about plans for a celebration.

"We're ready for a beer now," said Jeff Saunders of Manitouwadge.

Victory came around 1 p.m. yesterday when firefighters doused a final acre of burning rubber. That leaves only the mopping up of buried and isolated hot spots for today, officials said.

Meanwhile, officials are wondering why the Pentagon wants a day-by-day photo record of the war against the fire that started Feb. 12 at Ed Straza's tire dump.

It is not clear why the United States military needs the photographs, said Thomas.

He speculated the Pentagon is interested in the firefighting methods and strategy used to quell the massive blaze.

After dousing the last acre of burning tires yesterday, firefighters using infra-red heat detectors began inspecting the 4.6-hectare (11.5-acre) dump for hidden hot spots.

There's no telling how many hot spots will be found, and firefighters won't be able to go home until these are torn open and cooled, Thomas said.

The men will likely be demobilized at the end of the week, he said.

Denis Corr of the environment ministry praised those who had defeated the blaze, but cautioned that the fire's after-effects have only begun.

"In terms of the environment, we're not out of the woods yet — not by a very long way," he said.

About 567,810 kilograms (158,000 gallons) of oil, produced by melting tires, have been trucked from the site, he said.

Environment ministry tests done on 107 wells in the fire area show trace contamination in a handful of samples, he said.

Two wells had minute traces of benzene, and four of five showed evidence of toluene, Corr said.

But these were several kilometres away from the fire scene, and much closer wells were clean.

Meanwhile, refugees from the massive fire are making do in provincially funded mobile homes here.

Margaret Vandermeer, her husband, four daughters, two cats and a dog have moved into a mobile home. They were evacuated from their house, about 152 metres (500 feet) from the burning tire lot, on the first day of the fire.

"The kids think this is going to be great. It's a big adventure — fun stuff," Vandermeer said.

This style is frequent, and not only in journalism; it pervades business and professional writing. Notice how the result is more mosaic than sequence: many of the sentence-paragraphs can be moved around without disturbing the ideas. Note too how quickly the machine-gun prose moves by.

Characteristics

A series of one-sentence paragraphs has the same effect as a rapid series of snapshots or slides.

All of the snapshots are close-up: this kind of prose does not allow you detachment or perspective. It puts your nose six inches from the photo: you are deprived of aesthetic distance and plunged into the middle of the scene.

The sentence/paragraphs move by very quickly, so much so that the reader is afforded no time for reflection: such prose does not arouse the contemplative or meditative humors.

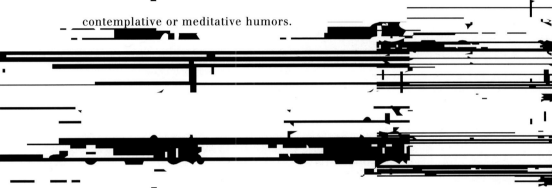

This rapid-fire, breathless style has little use for that mainstay of paragraph-writing, transitions. Consequently, writing composed of one-sentence paragraphs is more abrupt, non-linear, discontinuous – well-suited to conveying bare facts or impressions. Since it will also serve to communicate a "feel" and heighten emotion, advertisers like to use it to generate intensity, excitement. In addition, with this style a writer can assemble or present many points of view virtually simultaneously, in a discontinuous mosaic, so as to convey a whole situation or an overall sense or impression. The mosaic of points of view involves the reader in a process as it unfolds – from the inside, where all points of view converge.

In this style, because sentence and paragraph are merged, every sentence is a topic sentence. So there is no topic sentence and the paragraph

works like muzak: that is, it reverts from *figure* to *ground*. It is cubism in prose. Equally, it doesn't allow the writer to sustain a single focus: that is the special province of the developed paragraph.

While all four traditional sentence-structures (compound, complex, etc.) work well in this style, main clauses and (subordinate) noun clauses tend to predominate. Overall, average sentence length conforms to current norms of attention span.

Ordinarily (that is, in conventional prose), the one-sentence paragraph has two principal uses. First, it is used as a transition between larger elements of a presentation. "Having reviewed the main elements of the situation, I would like now to pass on to discussing their wider implications" – that sort of thing. Second, the brief, one-sentence paragraph has often been used for dramatic effect. "They all died." "The bomb exploded." "That's all she wrote."

And so on. Consequently, prose composed mainly or exclusively of one-sentence paragraphs combines these two characteristics: great mobility and great emotional impact. It goes like the wind and it hits hard. For that reason advertisers and journalists love it. Neither group strives to engage the higher reasoning faculties, and both aim for maximal excitement and concentrated impact.

Punch and power

The staccato style is a tough-as-nails, hard-hitting style. Each sentence / paragraph packs the punch of a paragraph into the space of a sentence: after all, it and the paragraph have merged. So it deploys the force of compressed statement. It hits the reader like a series of boxer's jabs: short, tight, rapid, powerful. But sustain it for too long and your reader will become punch-drunk. Therefore, it is best suited to presenting brief, newsy items, not to longer, essay-style writing.

The style itself is a pushy, assertive one: it shoves the reader around. In these terms the style works effectively whenever you need to assert your topic or yourself or your ascendancy over the reader. It also helps with emphatic (pushy) letters, memos, directives, etc. But it would not be a helpful style to employ when writing the longer essay or report, things which demand more leisurely, reflective paragraphs.

A particular word of caution about the verbs. In staccato style, avoid using more than a small percentage of copular (linking) verbs: they are bereft of energy and movement. A sustained series of staccato sentences built around copulas becomes amazingly static and saps energy from the reader. The prose lurches from idea to idea.

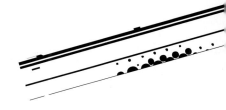

English has about thirty linking verbs: the verbs *to be* and *to become* are the foundation. Other common ones include *get, grow, turn, seem, appear, feel, smell, sound, look, taste.*

Variety

As the punchy staccato style will quickly numb the reader's sensibilities, the need for variety assumes great importance – at least in the editing process. Moreover, since sentence and paragraph have merged, "variety" demands every available device to vary that sentence. There are two principal ways to inject variety: by graphics and syntax.

Graphic variety can be introduced in three ways. One way, used occasionally (for example, in direct-mail pieces), involves varying the margins: indenting "paragraphs" at both left and right from time to time. A second way involves using headings to break up the text: heads and sub-heads establish another rhythm in the prose. Journalists excel at this technique and their efforts can be studied profitably. But there is a danger: headings are easy to overdo, so take the form of presentation into account. Will it be in narrow columns (as on a newspaper page) or in regular block (typewritten) format? If the latter, two or three heads per page of this style is adequate; if the former, every five to eight column inches provides a pleasant rhythm.

An additional feature of using headings: when used well, the heading can serve the same function as the topic sentence used to in the traditional paragraph – to focus the reader and lend coherence to what follows. The effect is of an exploded paragraph. But this style allows only one structure, inductive order: the topic must always be in the heading, at the top.

The alternative, oft-used in journalism and magazines, is to strew headings (made by "calling out" phrases from the text or by compressing provocative sentences) randomly throughout the writing. This device contributes to the mosaic feel of the piece and invites the reader to dip in and out. Headings, this way, are used for graphic and emotional impact and have no narrative function. They break the text into chunks that don't *look* forbiddingly long to the reader.

The most important means of varying involves sentence length and structure. Because sentence and paragraph have now merged, varying the length of sentence equals varying the size and weight of the paragraph. A few suggestions to keep in mind when using this style:

• Use all four types of sentence (simple, complex, compound, compound-complex).

• Deliberately play with emphasis: be more than usually conscious of the "pressure-points," at the beginning and end of the sentence: make both periodic and loose sentences. They are more potent at paragraph level.

• Make no more than half of your sentences of average length (2 lines of type). The rest need to be *visibly* shorter or longer: here, sentence length blends with graphics.

• Use the full range of available punctuation: semicolons, colons, etc. Too often, an unrelieved series of single-sentence paragraphs consists of simple, loose sentences with simple punctuation. The sheer simplicity and sustained repetition is deadening. Why not ask a question now and then? Parentheses are fine, too (though far more conspicuous here than in longer narrative paragraphs), but they're easily overdone.

Rhetorical Summary

1. Main uses of staccato style

- Summaries
- Overviews, Surveys
- Minutes of meetings
- Memos, E-mail
- Correspondence (most)
- Promotional literature
- Notes
- Outlining matters, situation
- Instructions (minus explanations)
- News writing

2. Not useful for

- Argument
- Reflective discussion
- Objective appraisal
- Analysis in depth
- Detailed description
- Continuous narrative
- Logical explication
- Causal discussion

3. Main forms of Organization

- Chronological order
- Order of importance
- Inverted pyramid
- Groups (of facts, impressions – between headings)

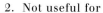

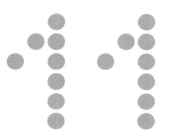

Two- and Three-sentence Paragraphs: Running Style

Sentence/paragraphs suit two kinds of reader: those with brief attention spans and those with a need to speed through a subject. The constant paragraph breaks, however, give such writing an abrupt, staccato character. So such writing presents a paradox: at once quick-moving, and static. But expand the "paragraph" slightly, to two or three sentences, and the static character recedes and a dramatic new style emerges: running style.

Normally, the larger the paragraph, the slower, more detailed, more reflective (and more objective) the prose. The reverse happens with running style. It retains many of the properties of the sentence/paragraph, yet can still move at breakneck pace. The extra sentence or two in each group makes the difference. Just as the length of a sentence is a measure of the reader's attention span, so too with the paragraph. As noted earlier, longer paragraphs such as those one- and two-pagers often found in nineteenth-century writing have quite disappeared from contemporary prose style.

Inside the small paragraph, one sentence, usually the first, announces the main theme and the other one or two amplify it or illustrate it or add detail. They prevent the prose from turning into a simple series of static close-ups. The four most frequent means of expanding the "lead" sentence in the group are these:

• Definition (of terms and ideas used in the lead sentence)

• Amplification: explain or give detail or examples

• Contrast or comparison

• Analogy: relate to something familiar or paraphrase in reader's terms

The theme sentence still works as a close-up, but the others move the reader back a little and contribute to the overall sense of motion.

Traditionally, the brief, two-sentence group amid sequences of developed paragraphs served to move the reader from larger topic to topic. Therefore, running style works best with active, transitive verbs: transitive for movement, active for energy.

That same motion and energy can heighten drama or intensify an emotion while it achieves great speed. As a result, the style is much used in news-writing and in sales-literature. Journalists want drama and impact (forget dry objectivity: no reader today is interested); sales demands energy and excitement to "pump up" the reader. But, as always, attaining high speed means sacrificing depth – the sort of thoughtful depth that 7- to 10-sentence paragraphs afford.

Rhythm

Every group of sentences must have a focus. *One* of the sentences must announce the business it and the others have in common: usually, that sentence carries the punch. As the reader speeds up, the emphases build up a rhythm. The "heavy hitter" (that is, the topic sentence) is frequently the first sentence in each group, so here is the result.

With two-sentence groups:

> STRONGlight,
>
> STRONGlight,
>
> STRONGlight,
>
> STRONGlight,
>
> STRONGlight,
>
> STRONGlight, etc. – the two-step!

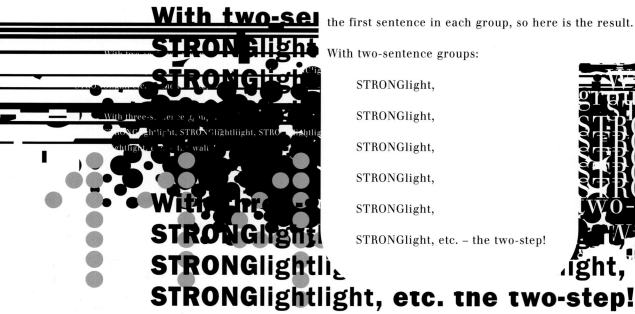

With three-sentence groups:

STRONGlightlight,

STRONGlightlight,

STRONGlightlight,

STRONGlightlight,

STRONGlightlight, etc. – the waltz!

When either rhythm establishes itself – it only takes three or four groups in a row – the reader will slide into, succumb to the rhythm, begin to doze off mentally. To avoid hypnotizing the reader, work at variety (usually in the editing process). At this juncture, the old science of metrics comes in to play in a new manner: the two-sentence paragraph offers a choice of structural iambs (– ´) or trochees (´ –); the three-sentence paragraph, of anapests (– – ´), dactyls (´– –), etc. Here, writ large, you can manage in a new medium the full spectrum of their effects and dynamic ranges, their strengths and weaknesses.

Variety

• Vary the rhythm by putting the punch (topic sentence) last, or middle, now and then.

• Vary rhythm by varying the number of sentences (one to five) in successive groups.

• Vary rhythm by using headings and sub-headings, irregularly spaced.

Rhetorical Summary

1. Uses of Running Style

- Reports

- Proposals

- Summaries

- Speeches

- All correspondence

- All memos, E-mail

- Minutes

- Instructions

- Manuals

- News writing

- Promotional literature

- Magazine articles

- Press releases

2. Not Useful For

- Detailed description

- Reflective discussion

- Analysis in depth

- Some cause/effect writing

3. Forms of Organization

- Pretty much the entire spectrum of choices suits running style

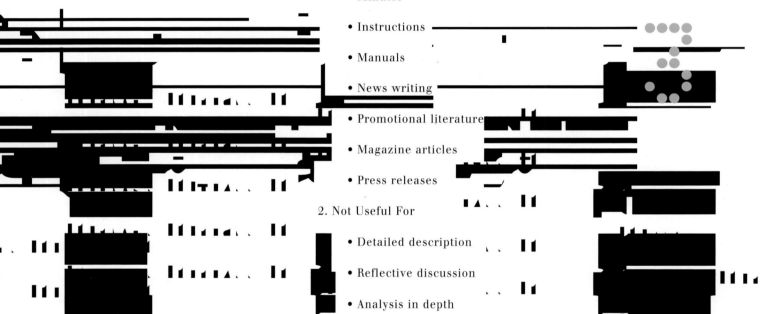

Point-Form Style: The End of the Sentence

Rhetorical summary

1. Main uses

 • Outlines

 • Executive summaries

 • Briefing notes

 • Memos

 • E-mail

 • Inventories, catalogues

2. Principal forms of Organization

 • Chronology

 • Order of Importance

 • Groups (by topic)

3. Not Useful For

 • Narrative prose

 • Argument

 • Logic

 • Detail, fill-in

 • Background

 • Depth, explanation

 • Description

4. Principal characteristics

 • Points are highly compressed: no extra words

 • Points do not exceed one – or at most two – sentences

 • Points do not even have to be full sentences (see above)

 • Points are not connected: no transitions

• Points do not include background fill or detail

• Points MUST be built in parallel: if one point in a group MUST be a sentence, so must the others, etc.

Remarks

Point-form style represents an unexpected revival, at grass-roots level. This new style exhibits one overriding feature: extreme economy and compression of statement. As a discontinuous inventory, or mosaic style, it moves in the direction of formal cause.

The point-form list is not a rearranged or compressed sentence, but a paragraph in miniature. It is the prose cartoon, but it is not prose. Nor is it a list, because the items do not necessarily depend from or connect to a heading. The one other area in our literary tradition that exercises the same parsimony with words is poetry. A poem should have no extra words the way a machine has no extra parts. Of course, that should be true of all good writing, but it is particularly true of poetry.

Point-form style would appear to have resurrected poetics in an unexpected form and an unexpected place, the business office. As yet it is without grace or aesthetic, subject only to the brute rule of economy, but the matrix is there, awaiting the soothing maieutic hand of the practiced obstetrician – the editor.

Graphics

Point-form style abruptly shifts the reader from the left side of the brain (sequential narrative) to the right side (imagery). In point-form presentation, then, clarity depends largely on graphics and layout. The conventional paragraph actually has no layout features: words and lines – like these –

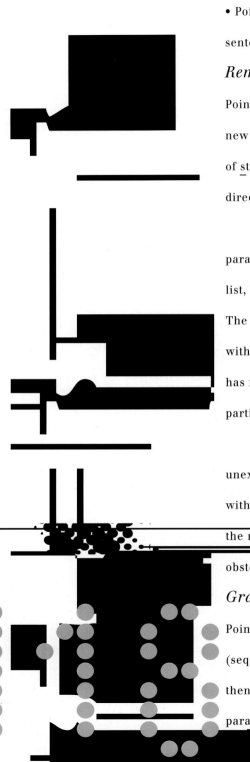

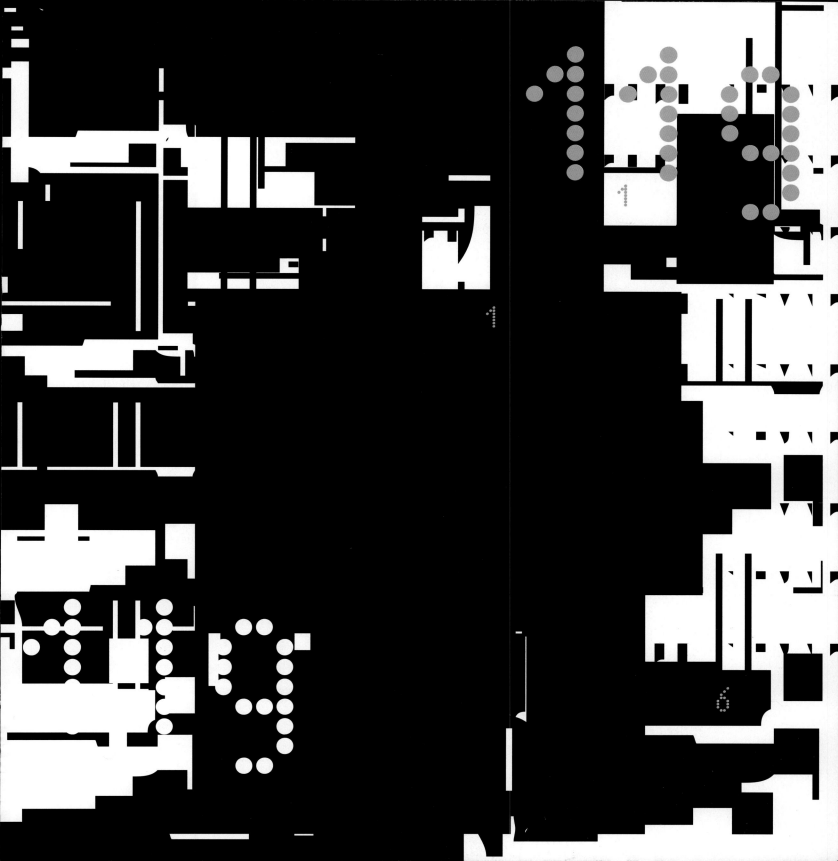

simply follow each other in regular procession. The sentence, and with it grammar and syntax, has little hold on point-form which routinely dispenses with all three. In their place it imposes the iron rule of parallelism (a kind of structural rhyming). The positions of headings, the amount of indentation, the darkness of font, of typeface or of bullets – all conduce to showing the importance of an item or significance of a list. Consistency and elegance of presentation generally matter more in this style than do the banal concerns of grammar and usage.

Here, now, a clear style that sheds that straightjacket, grammar. A muddle-crass, common, coarse, everyday, workaday style. A street-slang style. Pure poetics in the crucible.

To illustrate its currency as public style, here is an example from a magazine. The text below formed the entire closing article in *Canadian Forum*, April 1990, p. 32. Note the merging of point-form and staccato styles. Both styles are spare and like to work with facts.

Index On Native Canadians

by Pat Brascoupé and Georges Erasmus

- The Indian population of Canada is 466,337 of which 260,337 live on reserves.

- 164,000 reserve Indians (62%) live on social assistance.

- 120,000 off-reserve Indians (58%) are estimated to receive social assistance.

- In absolute terms, there are more Indians on social assistance than there are residents of the four Atlantic provinces combined on social assistance.

- Census data shows Native income to average little more than half (54%) of Canadian income.

- The people with the lowest average personal income ($10,382) are reserve Indians, one-half the Canadian average ($20,764).

- Native joblessness rates average nearly 70%.

- Out of a total federal government workforce of nearly 600,000 aboriginal participation is seven-tenths of one per cent, or 3,862, and no aboriginal women hold positions in the top salary range.

- Federal expenditures on Indian and Inuit programs have declined in real dollars by 11% over the last five years.

- The Indian population has increased by 33.7%.

- The life expectancy of male and female Indians will be over eight years lower than their Canadian counterparts in 1991.

- Indian infant mortality rates are more than double the Canadian rate (17.2 compared to 7.9 per 100 babies).

- Violent deaths in First Nation communities are nearly three times the national average (157 compared to 54.3 per 100,000 population).

- Over-crowding in reserve homes (about 30%) has risen to 16 times the Canadian rate (1.8%).

- Nearly 40% of reserve homes have no central heating, compared to only 5 % of Canadian homes.

- Indian children are four times more likely than Canadian children to be in the care of child welfare agencies.

- Functional illiteracy – those people with less than a grade nine education – for First Nations is 45% or two-and-a-half times the Canadian rate of 17%.

Pat Brascoupé is National Advisor at the Assembly of First Nations (AFN). Georges Erasmus is National Chief of the AFN.

Tetrad on Staccato Style: sentence/paragraph

Punch, foreground,
kinetic style
"breathless style"
snapshot, static, close-up

Pushes aside
depth
mosaic
kaleidoscope
speed

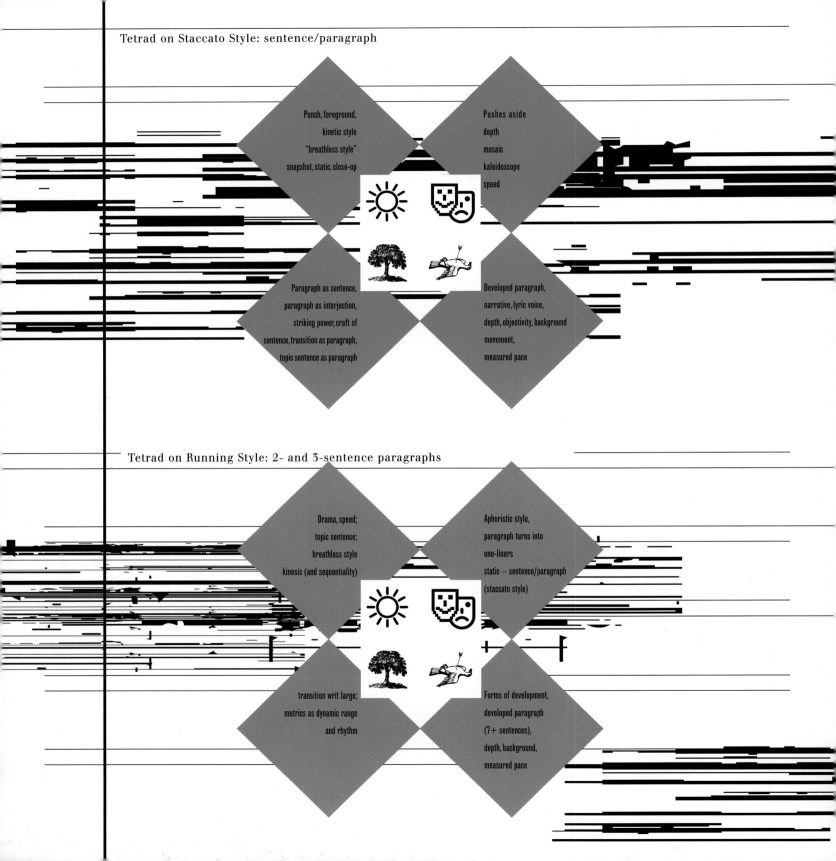

Paragraph as sentence,
paragraph as interjection,
striking power, craft of
sentence, transition as paragraph,
topic sentence as paragraph

Developed paragraph,
narrative, lyric voice,
depth, objectivity, background
movement,
measured pace

Tetrad on Running Style: 2- and 3-sentence paragraphs

Drama, speed;
topic sentence;
breathless style
kinesis (and sequentiality)

Aphoristic style,
paragraph turns into
one-liners
static — sentence/paragraph
(staccato style)

transition writ large;
metrics as dynamic range
and rhythm

Forms of development,
developed paragraph
(7+ sentences),
depth, background,
measured pace

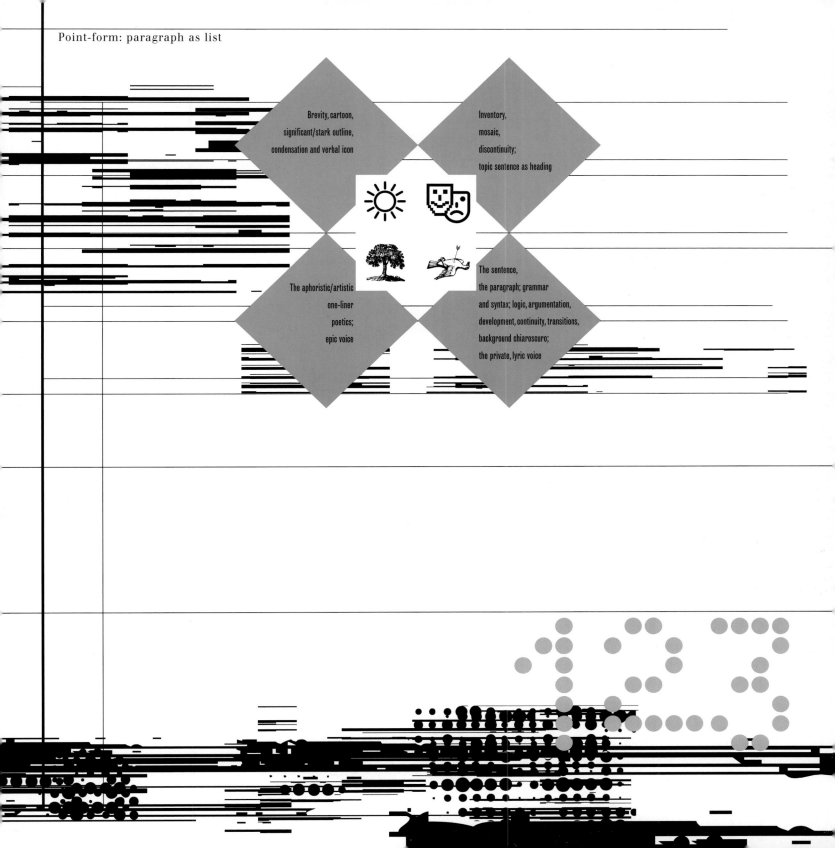

Brevity, cartoon,
significant/stark outline,
condensation and verbal icon

Inventory,
mosaic,
discontinuity;
topic sentence as heading

The aphoristic/artistic
one-liner
poetics;
epic voice

The sentence,
the paragraph; grammar
and syntax; logic, argumentation,
development, continuity, transitions,
background chiaroscuro;
the private, lyric voice

the reven of

Suicide as a Means of Survival

Remember the one about the Newfie "who committed suicide in self-defense"?
Today, increasing numbers are "committing suicide" as a way to survive the
irrational demands of the electric information environment.

Fifty years ago, Wyndham Lewis noted this tendency and described
its pathology, but people dismissed him as an alarmist. Lewis reported on
these matters in *Doom of Youth* and *The Art of Being Ruled.* His argument
in the former is simply this: when the adults refuse to grow up, they usurp
the territory formerly reserved for children. Having no means of combating
the encroachments of their elders, the kids must yield.

Nowadays, even while they sentimentalize childhood, the adults have
found a convenient weapon in their war against real children: they simply

declare as non-human those who threaten to encroach on their new-gained territory, a tactic that has served well in the past against all sorts of other inconvenient social groups. More recently, the battle has taken another turn: the new villain is every established moral or social norm, which are now declared evil because they are repressive. The immature cannot tolerate authority of any ilk. Lewis also appears to have foreseen the next phase of the war: abolishing the embarrassments of senility and old age by way of a sentimentalized euthanasia – presently called "dying with dignity." Meaning: death revitalized and refurbished as an aesthetic activity; death *à la mode*. Nothing that has appeared since on the subject has matched Lewis's acuity of both observation and insight:

Really what the "Doom of Youth" means is the erecting of "Youth" into a unique value, and by so doing abolishing Youth altogether. For something that is *everything* in human life cannot be anything so limited as "Youth" as understood upon the merely emotional plane.

A "Youth" (Peter Pan) *that never can grow up* – that is the *all-youth* of the super-sentimentalist. For him there is nothing whatever in the world of any value but "youth" in the traditionally romantic, the sugar-and-spice sense. "Youth-politician" – that is diametrically the opposite to Sir James Barrie's sickly variety, or the bogus and lisping species that is peculiar to the Invert's paradise.

For the "Youth-politician" there is, strictly speaking, *no youth*. There are only different degrees and powers of an abstract energy. There is one long *adult life*, if you like. No life is worth considering, for the "Youth-politician," except adult life. And adult life is not worth while, of course, once the person is no longer active and capable of creative or at least of useful work....

It is quite clear what is intended, and what is destined to come about. "Youth" is to be abolished altogether (just as the old "sex" conception was wiped out by Feminism). And it is also quite certain that it is the very reverse of that (to the mind of the simple Every-mans) which is on foot: nothing but endless, irresponsible, something-for-nothing "Youth" is their simplest of "Youth-politics." And, of course, for the *Everymans* it *will* be the reverse. – *Doom of Youth*, London: Chatto and Windus, 1932, p. 265

In a chapter reporting on "The Position of the Cult of *The Child* in the Present System," Lewis remarks, "I will interpolate here a brief account of how the *child* cult should be placed politically in relation to the attack on the family unit and the sex war. If you explained it entirely on the score of a defeated vitality, or of political eclipse, you would be mistaken, I think.

"The contributory causes of the cult of the child – in relation to the questions we have just been discussing – could be capitulated as follows: (1) Its usefulness as a kind of defeatist paradise for most of those accepting it: (2) its role as a factor in the 'sex war': and (3) its usefulness to those responsible for it and to some extent imposing it. It is obvious how closely it is related in that case with the wave of masculine inversion." – *The Art of Being Ruled*, London: Chatto and Windus, 1926, p. 285

Refusing to grow up constitutes a form of voluntary, psychic suicide or self-annihilation. Wrinkled Peter Pans – they surround us – are light-years removed from such attitudes as *dolce far niente* or even simple solipsism. Today's refusal to mature doesn't stem from laziness. It is a way to make time to adjust to current cultural conditions. However, it is worth noting that if healthy people are those who continue to grow and to mature throughout their lives, those that don't are, in effect, dead. Christopher Lasch wrote that "the distinction between the self and the not-self is the basis of all other distinctions, including the distinction between life and death....The narcissistic longing for fusion leads to a denial of both sexual and generational differences" (*The Minimal Self: Psychic Survival in Troubled Times* [New York and London: W. W. Norton, 1984], p.164). Westerners have for a generation now been immobilized by a massive paralysis of the mind and spirit at the stage of the infant, a paralysis inflicted by the swamping of rational, civilized culture by the electrified right hemisphere.

Although advertising has capitalized on this immaturity for decades and both encourages and sentimentalizes it, the advertisers are not to blame for the problem: they are just taking advantage of a condition that presents itself.

What you have to ask yourself is why, exactly, a grown person should wish to be a Child? – for to use the forms of infantile or immature life, to make an art of its technical imperfections, and to exploit its natural ignorance, is, in some sense, to wish to be a child. In writing of *The Art of Being Ruled* a year later, Lewis said, "How the *demented* also joins hands with the child, and the tricks, often very amusing, of the asylum patient, are exploited at the same time as the happy inaccuracies of the infant; how contemporary inverted-sex fashions are affiliated to the Child-cult; and in fact all the different factors in this intricate sensibility, being evolved notably by such writers as Miss Stein, will be found there. Not to seize the secret of these liaisons is to totally misunderstand the nature of what is occurring around you today." – *The Enemy: A Review of Art and Literature, Edited and Illustrated by Wyndham Lewis*, No. I (January 1927), Rpt., Santa Rosa, CA: Black Sparrow Press, 1994, pp. 75-76

Today, through ads, a child takes in all the times and places of the world "with his mother's TV." He is gray at three. By twelve he is a confirmed Peter Pan, fully aware of the follies of adults and adult life in general. These could be called Spock's Spooks, who now peer at us from every quarter of our world. Snoopy has put man on the moon and brought him back. Four years may already have become the upper limit of tolerable emotional maturity. – Marshall McLuhan, *Culture Is Our Business* (New York: McGraw-Hill, 1970), p. 7

"What is a 'sibling society'?" asks a blurb for a new book. "It is one in which adults have become squabbling children, in which fathers have jumped ship, mothers are poised to jump and what we are left with is the 'Providing Mother' of television, the lay temple of the suburban shopping mall and those two fatherless sons, Bill Clinton and Newt Gingrich, competing for approval." (Blurb from the *Book of the Month Club News* flyer, July 1996, on Robert Bly's book *The Sibling Society*. By the time any malaise, social or cultural, hits the popular bookshelves, it has to be pretty advanced.) The Good Ship Lollipop has become the Ship of State.

Maturity, in Western culture, meant cultivating both a private identity and a facility with detached and rational single points of view. An environment of information moving at electric speed in all directions simultaneously makes such things as fixed points of view irrelevant and impossible to sustain. The sensitive organism instinctively shrinks from such antiquated folly as a fixed private self, in the interests of sheer self-preservation.

With the new technologies, "the line between the living and the dead has been growing increasingly vague," writes Mark Slouka. "Every day old frontiers are being erased or pushed back; every year, in laboratories throughout the

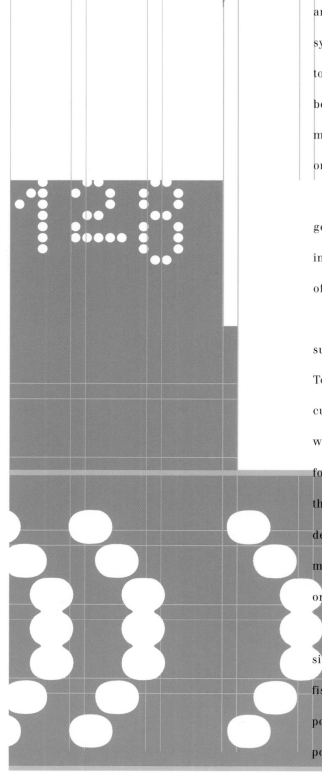

industrialized world, the edges blur. Already, some of the characteristics of life are being transferred to mechanical systems, even as the engineering of organic systems is progressing at staggering speeds: from baboon hearts to biopesticides to the bovine growth hormone, we're learning to 'hack life.' Soon, the distinction between technologized life (that's us) and living technology (our environment) may be lost forever." – War of the Worlds: Cyberspace and the High-tech Assault on Reality (New York: Harper Collins/ Basic Books, 1995), p.67

Surprisingly, our current Peter Pan and Mother Goose do not represent genuine Narcissism, but rather the reverse: they present the exact mirror-image of a Narcissus. The story of Narcissus is an allegory of the romance of integral man with outward mechanical projections of himself.

The big side-effect of the machine in the garden was carried in the sub-plot – the death of Echo, that is, the suppression of the right hemisphere. Today, however, the love-affair surges not outward but inward, on electric current. Christopher Lasch and the Narcissism-analysts have it exactly back-wards. Although the new condition may resemble that of Narcissus, even point for point, it is the mirror-image or echo-form, the revenge of Echo, that has them hypnotized. No more is Echo a babe in the woods. Since her original demise, she has merged with the Gorgon sisters and re-emerged as, among many other forms, the feminist storm-trooper and the messianic promoter or priestess of the "postmodern" New Age.

Private will (and its complement, the ability to shoulder private respon-sibility) and private identity (and its complement, individual privacy) are fission by-products of the phonetic alphabet. In putting on the abstracting power of the alphabet, the user also puts on individual awareness and private points of view. Similarly, today's paralyzed Pan dramatizes, by living as if already dead, the action of his electric environment.

By making the right hemisphere the pattern of the environment, electric media instill simultaneity, involvement, and imagery as our mode of sensibility. Ordinary experience acquires mythic dimensions because it is multi-leveled. The consequent obsolescence of sequentiality means also the negating of simple chronology: all-time is instantaneously present, all ages and historical periods past and present, now; effects precede causes; distant goals and objectives, and all mere things, become ephemera. History ends.

Lasch: "Narcissism emerges as the typical form of character structure in a society that has lost interest in the future." As history and the future are obsolesced, enter the futurologists and social engineers and designers of futures for everyman. "Psychiatrists who tell parents not to live through their offspring; married couples who postpone or reject parenthood, often for good practical reasons; social reformers who urge zero population growth, all testify to a pervasive uneasiness about reproduction – to widespread doubts, indeed, about whether our society should reproduce itself at all. Under these conditions the thought of our eventual supersession and death becomes utterly insupportable and gives rise to attempts to abolish old age and to extend life indefinitely. When men find themselves incapable of taking an interest in earthly life after their own death, they wish for eternal youth, for the same reason they no longer care to reproduce themselves. When the prospect of being superseded becomes intolerable, parenthood itself, which guarantees that it will happen, appears almost as a form of self-destruction."

– *The Culture of Narcissism: American Life in an Age of Diminishing Expectations* (New York: Warner Books, 1979), p. 357

Grow up? Sixty years ago, James Joyce wrote, in *Finnegans Wake*, that

Here is the story, from Ovid's *Metamorphoses*

Once, when Narcissus was sixteen, and was out hunting with friends, he was espied by the nymph Echo, "who could neither hold her peace when others spoke nor yet begin to speak till others had addressed her....When she saw Narcissus wandering through the fields, she was inflamed with love and followed him by stealth; and the more she followed the more she burned by a nearer flame." But she could not bring herself to approach him and declare her ardor. She approaches him and he flees. "Thus spurned, she lurks in the woods, hides her shamed face among the foliage, and lives from that time on in lonely caves. But still, though spurned, her love remains and grows on grief; her sleepless cares waste away her wretched form; she becomes gaunt and wrinkled and all moisture fades from her body into the air. Only her voice and her bones remain: then, only her voice; for they say that her bones were turned to stone. She hides in woods and is seen no more upon the mountain-sides; but all may hear her, for her voice, and voice alone, still lives in her.

"Thus had Narcissus mocked her, thus had he mocked other nymphs of the waves or mountains; thus had he mocked the companies of men....There was a clear pool with silvery bright water, to which no shepherds ever came, or she-goats feeding on the mountain-side, or any other cattle; whose smooth surface neither bird nor beast nor falling bough ever ruffled. Grass grew all around its edge, fed by the water near, and a coppice that would never suffer the sun to warm the spot. Here the youth, worn by the chase and the heat, lies down, attracted thither by the appearance of the place and by the spring. While he seeks to slake his thirst another thirst springs up, and while he drinks he is smitten by the sight of the beautiful form he sees. He loves an unsubstantial hope and thinks that substance which is only shadow. He looks in speechless wonder at himself and hangs there motionless in the same expression, like a statue carved from Parian marble. Prone on the ground, he gazes at his eyes, twin stars, and his locks, worthy of Bacchus, worthy of Apollo; on his smooth cheeks, his ivory neck, the glorious beauty of his face, the blush mingled with snowy white; all things, in short, he admires for which he is himself admired. Unwittingly he desires himself; he praises, and is himself what he praises; and while he seeks, is sought; equally he kindles love and burns with love. How often did he offer vain kisses on the elusive pool? How often did he plunge his arms into the water seeking to clasp the neck he sees there, but did not clasp himself in them! What he sees he knows not, but that which he sees he burns for, and the same delusion mocks and allures his eyes. O fondly foolish boy, why vainly seek to clasp a fleeting image? What you seek is nowhere, but turn yourself away, and the object of your love will be no more. That which you behold is but the shadow of a reflected form and has no substance of its own. With you it comes, with you it stays, and it will go with you – if you can go.

"No thought of food or rest can draw him from the spot; but, stretched on the shaded grass, he gazes on that false image with eyes that cannot look their fill and through his own eyes perishes. Raising himself a little, and stretching his arms to the trees, he cries: 'Did anyone, O ye woods, ever love more cruelly than I? You know, for you have been the convenient haunts of many lovers. Do you in the ages past, for your life is one of centuries, remember one who has pined away like this? I am charmed, and I see; but what I see and what charms me I cannot find – so great a delusion holds my love. And to make me grieve the more, no mighty ocean separates us, no long road, no mountain ranges, no city walls with close-shut gates; by a thin barrier of water we are kept apart...'" Narcissus goes on in like manner for some time, yet cannot tear himself away from his reflection. Eventually, he wastes away and dies on the spot. "And even when he had been received into the infernal abodes, he kept on gazing on his image in the Stygian pool." Eventually, his naiad-sisters began preparing the funeral pile, the brandished torches and the bier; but his body was nowhere to be found. In place of his body they find a flower, its yellow centre girt with white petals" – the Narcissus. (Book III, lines 351-510)

the average man was "grey at three." That is, by that age he had encountered more experience than his grandparents in an entire lifetime lived at a slower pace. Half a century later, in an environment of information even further accelerated, there is not more impulse to mature, but less; there is literally nowhere to go. We are all nearly stillborn. Ponce de Leon's supposition that the fountain of youth was located in some far-off land reflected the outer-directed, left-brain bias of his time and culture: today, everyman goes wildcatting in Bimini, deep inside the group-self.

Once, when we were a civilized people (that is, a people based on the *civis*, the private citizen), only royalty and the very rich were afflicted by this disease. All of the goals or aspirations of these people had been met before they were born. With nowhere new to go, nothing new to do, the only occupation left to them was that of growing up. In our time, with Peter Pan and Mother Goose the popular patterns of being, the newest and most important form of social activity in our culture may well become mere maturing. Adults in some form or other may become necessary, if only to tend the nursery. But with every hand against you, with the whole environment pushing in the opposite direction, maturing is now not only tough, but hazardous as well. The mature individual is now with increasing frequency being declared a social misfit. Disguise is already essential. In the age of the disappearance of jobs, as a cultural activity of the first importance, growing up should be paid, subsidized work.

Death as a way of life is a paradox only for rational people: it has long been used as a technique of survival in the East. As Ruth Benedict reported a generation ago, it was a recommended strategy, often the only viable one, for attaining excellence. (See *The Chrysanthemum and the Sword: Patterns of Japanese Culture* [Cleveland and New York: Meridian Books, 1967], pp. 249-

251, 289-290.) Live as if already dead, and no mortal failing, no personal fear or inadequacy, no social pressure, no worldly obstacle can prevent you from attaining your objective. Eastern and oriental cultures find no paradox in this advice. It strikes only Western, literate sensibilities as bizarre. We had to *invent* the phenomenological reduction and its social expression, punk: a commonplace of all Eastern mysticism is that the world and its contents are not "real" but are mere manifestations of a lower order of consciousness. The Cyberspace prophets are ahead of the rank and file users of computers and gadgets: they already regard RL (real life) as illusory and a hindrance to their explorations:

To say that the real world didn't interest the cyberists, however, wasn't quite accurate; they didn't *believe* in it. "What we call reality," Stegner explained, "is only a temporary consensus anyway, a mere stage in the technique." Bodies, Professor Heim claimed, didn't really exist, either: they were ideological constructs – composites of attitudes, beliefs, and preconceptions, themselves dependent on larger economic and political forces at work in the general culture. Nature, too, was merely an idea, a cultural construct. Like love. Or gender." – Slouka, *War of the Worlds*, p. 31

When the inner landscape becomes the life-world, as with Virtual Reality or as on the Internet, all manner of other reversals occur. The patriarchy of hardware – tangible things – yields to the matriarchy of software – imagery and information. The outer world, with its pressures and demands, becomes the enemy; so too does anything that threatens to haul one back to outer

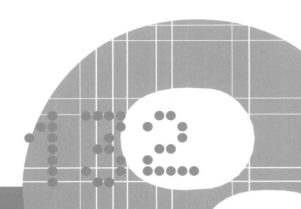

"A new consciousness is rising," June Singer announces in *Androgyny*, a "feminine consciousness" that rejects individualism, separation, "logical thinking," and "linear reasoning." The old ego-centered psychology is yielding to a "holistic" psychology that sees the self as part of an ecological continuum, a "vast over-all plan" (*The Minimal Self*, p. 250). Singer is but one of a horde blinded by the new technologies and robotically obeying their dictates to embrace the right hemisphere and to discard the left and all its civilized attributes: this is the new barbarism. The past – history – is first trivialized, then subjected to attack, and finally rejected outright.

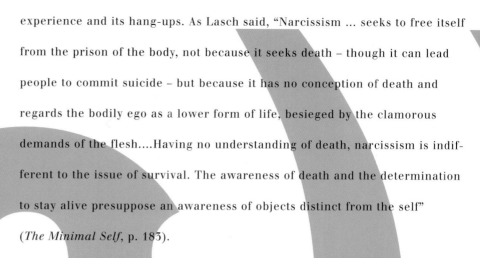

experience and its hang-ups. As Lasch said, "Narcissism ... seeks to free itself from the prison of the body, not because it seeks death – though it can lead people to commit suicide – but because it has no conception of death and regards the bodily ego as a lower form of life, besieged by the clamorous demands of the flesh....Having no understanding of death, narcissism is indifferent to the issue of survival. The awareness of death and the determination to stay alive presuppose an awareness of objects distinct from the self" (*The Minimal Self*, p. 183).

To the dead, life is a purely aesthetic trip; it is a form of absurd theater. The outer world and its contents are allowed only the salience and reality that can be conferred on them without playing the inner world false. The outside is small, tainted, and circumscribed by matter. The exciting discovery is that we are immensely larger on the inside that we are on the outside. The inner sphere of fantasy is a mythic and discontinuous world of simultaneous relations and sudden, magical transformations. It embraces all places and all times and cultures and forms of experience, not private, single consciousness.

Is it just coincidence or is it irony of mythic proportions that the phenomenologists discovered the "life-world" at just the moment that the real world was being remade by fantasy into a stage re-populated electronically by robots, zombies, and avatars? These characters are themselves the fallout

And do not call it fixity,
Where past and future are gathered. Neither movement
from nor towards,
Neither descent nor decline...
Time past and time future
Allow but a little consciousness.
To be conscious is not to be in time...
involved with past and future.
– T. S. Eliot, *Four Quartets*, "Burnt Norton," II

from electric implosion of the literate psyche. They dramatize and allegorize in their everyday lives what happens when a culture originally formed on the pattern of mechanical extensions is translated into electric information.

Peter Pan, the eternal youth, is in real life a death-cult nihilist. Minus physical roots in the outside world, minus any possibility of private identity, he also lacks the basis for forming social or even sexual identity. The "child" as we know it was an invention of the seventeenth century: prior to that time there was no distinction made between, say, a child's world and that of the adult: all existed in the one (adult) world. Now we have the spectacle of the disappearance of childhood as the adults take over the nursery.

Neil Postman concluded that television erodes the line dividing childhood and adulthood in several ways. "The new media environment that is emerging provides everyone, simultaneously, with the same information. Given the conditions I have described, electric media find it impossible to withhold any secrets. Without secrets, of course, there can be no such thing as childhood" (*The Disappearance of Childhood.* New York: Dell, 1982, p. 80). Postman thought that the computer would sustain the need for childhood: he did not foresee that it would have precisely the reverse effect. In his terms, it further abolishes secrets and vastly increases the environmental pressure of information. After the sixteenth century, widespread literacy fostered the notion of the child as a separate kind of human with a different nature and different needs. Children were separated from the general population "because it became essential in their culture that they learn how to read and write and how to be the sort of people a print culture required.... Where literacy was valued highly and persistently, there were schools, and where there were schools, the concept of childhood developed rapidly" (pp. 38-39). The computer screen has no more use for literacy than does the television screen: the alphabet belongs to an earlier and slower medium. It is the least efficient and least satisfying imaginable use of the screen.

Today's hard-core Pan is pre-pubescent, paralyzed at the stage of infant, insistent on his absolute right to remain infantile, insistent too on his right to wield the absolute power proper to all infants. In time this *enfant terrible* may drift to either extreme, the terrorist or the "adult" prodigy (which has lately replaced the child prodigy). Both are professional nobodies. Of the two, the terrorist is probably the more benign form, because it is conspicuous. The second is the more insidious because it is so commonplace. Examples litter the talk shows and game shows and sit-coms, hollow husks and professional "personalities," people well-known for being famous, distinguished only by an excess of some ordinary human trait or foible.

135

Early in his career, James Joyce noted that the hardware form of society, the city, was "the centre of paralysis." In the light of our present-day pandemic agèd pre-pubescence, and given such a tip-off, surely any civilized government would rush to expend massive amounts in the interests of preserving a little civilization (or just in the selfish interest of self-preservation) to investigate this observation. At least Canadians might form a Royal Commission to learn whether there are any babes in the woods – that is whether or not infantilist paralysis is confined to the cities, or whether it accompanies the infestation of an entire culture by the Internet.

The average person has become Petrified. Stunned. Stoned. Astonished. He has no articulate reply to infant sex-terrorists gleefully proclaiming and promoting the equality of all variations: bisexual, lesbian, homosexual, heterosexual, unisexual, asexual, animal. Any hesitation or reluctance is promptly scorned or denigrated (e.g., as "homophobic" or as antiquated and politically incorrect). At the asexual nursery-stage it's all one, anyway. That the differences between one mode and another have merely aesthetic significance is an attitude only possible to an androgynous population. Chemical contraception has played its part here: it is a form of street-theater. This environmental con-fusion of sexual identities is replayed and reprocessed endlessly as nothing more sinister than physiological aesthetics.

Electricity turns the body into an aesthetic object in several ways. Out-of-body, discarnate experience is a normal *ground*-feature of all who live in an electric milieu. On the telephone or on the air, the user functions minus a physical body: so the body is a quaint hangover of an earlier age, completely irrelevant to the electric wedding of central nervous systems. In this manner, we sever all allegiance to natural law and all relation to any cultural, social,

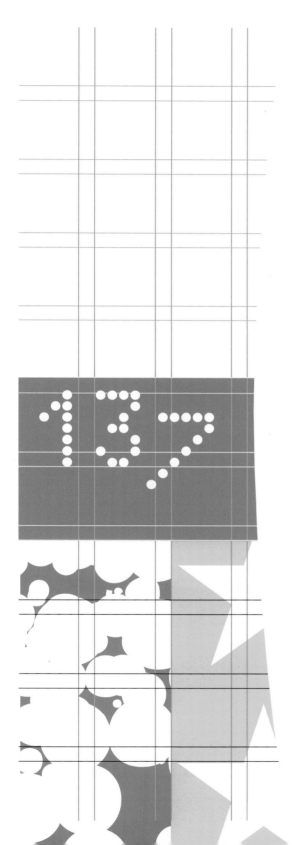

or psychic forms rooted in outward experience. While the outer world is rendered fantastic and unreal, the inward fantasy world is rendered real. The old "real world" is permeated by becoming and decay: it is matter, not pure, not spirit, not intuitive. Ignoring or bypassing it – by preferring the life of the Great Within, for example – is the same as destroying it. When we are grounded in the body, the world is real; when we live out of the body, the world turns paranormal.

Sooner or later, in one form or another, the outer world must be annihilated by these new discarnate types: their survival depends upon it. Each one performs his own annihilation. The world demands of us fixity, identity, stability, and responsibility – of the old-fashioned, unwelcome type. Needless to say, identity, whether private or sexual, is not possible unless matter and spirit converge, unless outer realities are retained as the *ground* of being. The discarnate being is Protean, sexless, endlessly transforming and mutable, mythic. Lacking an outer world and the outward goals that accompany it, we have flipped to inner "goals," evinced in the emphasis during the last decade or so on "self-actualization." Self-actualization is an endless process of "discovery" and transformation (right-brain) that replaces (left-brain) fixed individual identity. The collapse of private identity is documented in Lasch's work, and in such recent studies as *If I'm So Successful, Why Do I Feel Like a Fake?: The Impostor Phenomenon* by Harvey and Katz (New York: St. Martin's Press, 1985) and *Living Without a Goal: Finding the Freedom to Live a Creative and Innovative Life* by James Ogilvy (New York: Doubleday/ Currency Books, 1995).

Peter Pan, the average guy, is committed to preserving the nothingness of matter and of materialists. When the devotees of eternal Youth worship at

What did he do! what did he do?

That don't apply.

Talk to live men about what they do.

He used to come and see me sometimes.

I'd give him a drink and cheer him up.

Cheer him up?

SWEENEY: Well here again that don't apply
But I've gotta use words when I talk to you.
But here's what I was going to say.
He didn't know if he was alive
    and the girl was dead
He didn't know if the girl was alive
    and he was dead
He didn't know if they both were alive
    or both were dead
If he was alive then the milkman wasn't
    and the rent-collector wasn't
And if they were alive then he was dead.
There wasn't any joint
There wasn't any joint
For when you're alone
When you're alone like he was alone
You're either or neither
I tell you again it don't apply
Death or life or life or death
Death is life and life is death
I gotta use words when I talk to you
But if you understand or if you don't
That's nothing to me and nothing to you
We all gotta do what we gotta do
We're gonna sit here and drink this booze
We're gonna sit here and have a tune
we're gonna stay and we're gonna go
And somebody's gotta pay the rent

DORIS: I know who

SWEENEY: But that's nothing
to me and nothing to you.

–T. S . Eliot, "Fragment of an Agon"

the occult shrine deep within, they automatically turn to death-cults and the aesthetics of death as a way of life and a right to be asserted.

Sweeney is an amphibian, living on the border between the outer and inner worlds.

One immediate side-effect on a Westerner of escaping from private identity is a surge of personal and social violence. The forms are legion, from violence in the family (abortion, child-, wife- and husband-beating; gassing granny – euthanasia – or just relegating her to a "home") to violence in the street or the clash of armies. Give Pan a machine gun and he turns up as a terrorist. It is no paradox that, living the life within, the terrorist often discovers divine or spiritual motives for his or her mission of death and mayhem. All war in an environment of electric information becomes holy war – from terrorism to masochism.

The androgynous within-crowd of petrified Pans is the natural enemy of healthy, effervescent, outer-directed youth. The real child must somehow be suppressed or drugged, by chemicals or media (if it can't be killed or aborted in time). There is no real paradox or contradiction in the double pressure on youth nowadays – to remain babies as long as possible (so as not to threaten adult Pans) and to skip childhood entirely. Youth is doomed, wrote Lewis half a century ago. Childhood is, from now on, an adult preserve. No poaching. In the New Age, a child is acceptable only as an aesthetic object.

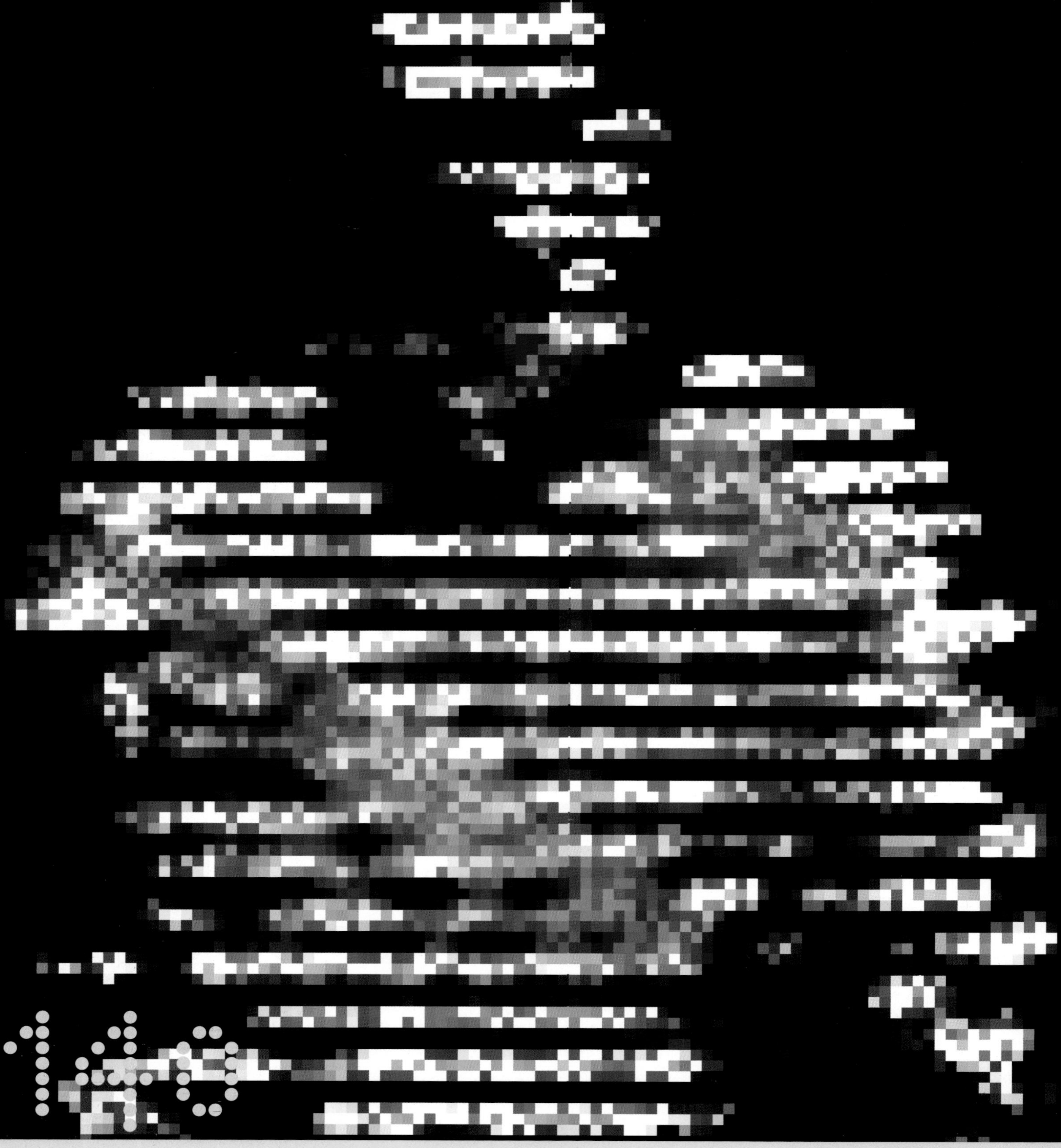

Anatomy of the Electric Crowd

A crowd flowed over London Bridge, so many
I had not thought death had undone so many.
–T. S. Eliot, *The Waste Land*, I,
"The Burial of the Dead"

In *Crowds and Power*, Elias Canetti revealed that there are just two basic forms of crowd: open and closed. The open crowd is everywhere spontaneous. It is programmed with a need to grow, and it has a terror of stagnating or getting smaller.

> As soon as it exists at all, it wants to consist of more people: the urge to grow is the first and supreme attribute of the [open] crowd. It wants to seize everyone within reach; anything shaped like a human being can join it. The natural crowd is the open crowd; there are no limits whatever to its growth; it does not recognize houses, doors or locks and those who shut themselves in are suspect. "Open" is to be understood here in the fullest sense of the word; it means open everywhere and in any direction. The open crowd exists so long as it grows; it disintegrates as soon as it stops growing.... – Elias Canetti, *Crowds and Power*. Translated from the German by Carol Stewart. (New York: Viking Penguin, 1963. Rpt. Peregrine Books, 1987), p.17

The closed crowd is marked by stability:

> The closed crowd renounces growth and puts the stress on permanence. The first thing to be noticed about it is that it has a boundary. It established itself by accepting its limitation... the important thing is always the dense crowd in the closed room; those standing outside do not really belong. The boundary prevents disorderly increase, but it also makes it more difficult for the crowd to disperse and so postpones its dissolution. – *Ibid*., p. 17

Mysteriously, the human crowd is the same everywhere, in all times and cultures, regardless of language or even of education. All of the manifestations of the crowd that we experience daily, with one exception, are either open

crowds or closed crowds. A group of idlers, pedestrians in a mall or on a sidewalk, passengers on a bus or airplane – these are not yet crowds. Those people still retain their individuality and are aware of it. Something has yet to occur which will suddenly forge the crowd from the raw material of assorted individuals and involve them in the vortex of corporate being and power. Before this the crowd does not actually exist. This is the moment of discharge, the moment when all who belong to the crowd get rid of their differences and feel equal. Think, for example, of a group of people at a concert or in a theater and what happens to it the moment the curtain rises. Suddenly the attention of each and every member focuses on a single event and the group becomes one.

But one mode of the crowd, the one exception mentioned above, is Canetti's most significant omission: the crowd we sometimes call the mass audience. He did discuss various audiences as crowds – for example, the crowd in a stadium or arena – but he did not mention the crowd that attends a radio show or TV program, etc., the electric crowd. Although it has some of the attributes he discovers in open and closed crowds, the electric crowd actually constitutes a third form, distinct from the other two. It has four main attributes.

All mass audiences are electric crowds, and vice-versa. Sheer speed creates the mass: at electric speed all bathe in the same matter simultaneously, thereby circumventing privacy and detachment (objectivity). A public, on the other hand, is characterized by individualized experience and detachment of outlook.

Basic Relativity: as a particle approaches the speed of light, its mass increases towards infinity and its size decreases towards zero. Speed

translates into mass, and vice-versa: this confirms the first attribute.

All mass audiences, regardless of numbers, are the same size. How many angels can dance on the head of a pin? How big an electric crowd can dance in a diode? On an electron? By this property, they are exempt from the open crowd's need constantly to grow. Yet they are not in any conventional sense closed crowds.

Everyone in a mass audience becomes everyman, that is, a no-body. Anonymous equals unanimous: electric crowds are absolutist and (like electric media) monarchical, not democratic. Electric media – telegraph, telephone, radio, television, computer, record- or tape- or CD-player – extend the central nervous system and bypass the body; they make the body irrelevant, obsolete as a means of distinguishing one person from another.

St. Thomas Aquinas pointed out that the principle of individuation, of individual identity, is "materia signata," matter "signed with" spirit – the coming-together of matter and spirit, the confluence of a mind and a body. Because **all members of every electric crowd are disembodied, discarnate,** "the discharge" occurs instantaneously and automatically, as a side-effect of using any electric medium. Without the body, there are neither individuals nor individual differences to discard. And because of electric speed, there is no preliminary build-up or waiting period.

Paradoxically, the experience of the crowd is the negative of the reality. The member of an incarnate open or closed crowd has the feeling of losing individualism (the emotion called *darshan*), but the member of the discarnate electric crowd feels as if individualism is intact.

The electric discharge results in corporate identity: minus the body, there remains nothing on which to base private awareness or private experience. As a corollary to the old axiom of mathematics that things equal to the same thing are equal to each other, there is this one: people who participate in the same thing at the same time participate in each other. Whether or not that participation is conscious or unconscious, it has the *effect* of negating private experience and creating an electric crowd. Discarnate participation equals what Canetti's incarnate crowds experience as the "discharge."

It's easy to see that these things apply to broadcast media, but what to make of an experience such as watching a video? Electric media all sidestep rational space and time; they substitute simultaneity for sequentiality and detachment. On the net or web, as on the air by means of radio or TV, the user is everywhere at once. Living at electric speed, all times are now, so we have "the end of history": history as we know it is a thing of the past. A few dozen –

or hundred or thousand – at a time may see a video of a film, but all of them together constitute its crowd and participate in it and each other electronically.

Canetti came perilously close (but no cigar) to identifying the electric crowd in his discussion of "invisible crowds." His first example of an invisible crowd was what we have lately referred to as "the great silent majority," a term Homer used for the dead.

Over the whole earth, wherever there are men, is found the conception of the invisible dead. It is tempting to call it humanity's oldest conception. There is certainly no horde, no tribe, no people which does not have

146

abundant ideas about its dead....

They were generally thought of as being together, just as men are together, and generally it was assumed that there were a great many of them... It could be argued that religions begin with these invisible crowds. (Canetti, pp. 47, 51)

Another invisible crowd, one that presses on us constantly, we call posterity. Still others include germs and bacilli, and the crowd of spermatozoa. I think, too, we must reckon as crowds the rapidly multiplying number of television channels suddenly available, and the environmental glut of information now burgeoning on the several networks and webs.

When one has available only one or two TV channels, they function rather as a closed crowd does, but when the number escalates to 30 or 100 or 500, as is now happening, they exert the same psychic pressures as an open crowd: they generate a need to get larger and at the same time they give the feeling of shrinking. The user reacts to these pressures with a sort of hysteria manifested as a need to view all of the channels at once: the result is the channel surfer. A similar phenomenon occurs with the computer-information webs and networks and accounts in some degree for their evident addictivness. "Knowledge is a drug on the market," observed the poet, Ezra Pound, over sixty years ago; yes, and information is an intensely addictive drug.

Certainly, the electric crowd is invisible, beyond detection by bodily senses because it lives apart from its bodies. In terms of ordinary human scale, the only time the mind or spirit parts from the body is at death, so to use electric media is to adopt – to put on – death as the mode of experience. Doing so must be utterly disorienting; in other words, it calls for a radical adjustment of attitude to incarnate existence. Perhaps this fact accounts for

the current fascination with the end-points of human life, the entry and exit points, and the public's new insistence on the "right" to manipulate them aesthetically (that is, qualitatively) by means of abortion and euthanasia. If the dead constitute an invisible crowd, so do those conceived but not yet born; and they, who are assuming bodies for the first time, do seem to present a potent, even deadly threat to those who have shed their bodies electrically. The burgeoning baby, in the absence of parental sentimentalism (which kicks in after it is born), turns into absolute monster, one that drags the parents kicking and screaming back into the world of bodies and of bodily imperfections. Equally, the current push for euthanasia is made entirely on aesthetic grounds: dying is being made into an art form, a programmable activity. Dying "with dignity" means dying *à la mode*. Nothing in the entirety of prior human experience has prepared us to adapt to these electric circumstances.

The electric crowd lives as if already dead: no wonder increasing numbers find nihilism a natural outlook. There is no reason whatever to assume that dabbling in discarnate existence is in any way beneficial for otherwise rational, living humans. Canetti noted that there are "crystals" that serve to precipitate crowds. A speaker or a group of actors in a play can serve as a crystal, or an orchestra, or opposing sports teams. Role-playing characterizes the crystal, whether individual or group, and the roles must be familiar: doubt about their function would render them meaningless.

The crowd crystal is constant; it never changes its size. Its members... may be allotted different parts, as in an orchestra, but they must appear as a unit, and the first feeling of anyone seeing or experiencing them must be that this is a unit which will never fall apart. Their life outside the crystal does not count. (Canetti, p. 85)

The famous Nazi propaganda film, *Triumph of the Will*, is about a crowd crystal (the speakers) and its crowds.

The *ground* for THE electric crowd is the totality of electric media present and operating. The *ground* for AN electric crowd is A medium. So we have the radio crowd, the TV crowd, the telegraph crowd, the Internet crowd, even the telephone crowd. **"The show" serves as the crowd crystal.**

Electric crowds are para-natural: they have transcended being-in-the-body for sheer being, in the absolute.

The electric crowd can have no goal distant in time or space to achieve, no objective, no quarry. Such goals are pointless and irrelevant because electric speed abridges all distances and separations in space and time. Its focus, as a crowd, is all inward: no outer "reality" residue remains after the body has been left behind. It simply IS. **Being is not an objective or a goal.**

A consequence of the last several points: An electric crowd finds significance or consequence only in quality of being, modality of being. Being cannot be quantified; hence our society's shift in emphasis, over the last couple of decades, to quality of life. People have no idea why they suddenly shifted to quality of this or that: it just seemed the right thing to do. In other words, we are disoriented, floundering. Each electric medium does not so much extend the bodily senses as it extends into the environment or around the world a parody or prosthesis of the central nervous system itself. So each new electric technology represents one or another modulation of being: herewith the foundation of all mass-audience aesthetics.

A further consequence: our established notions of consciousness all relate to incarnate experience; is it paradox that the form of consciousness proper to an electric crowd, i.e., to knowing outside the body, is un-consciousness?

That is, what the electric crowd knows is itself...in a tacit or unconscious manner. It "knows" with the unconscious. So it is no surprise that advertising in the last two decades has shifted its emphasis from selling products to supplying imagery and corporate identities for the users. Hence, too, the popularity of vacuous sit-coms, which serve as crowd crystals. The more vacuous the better, because the less the content, the less the demand on the rational conscious and the more energy the users can devote to unconscious participation.

Attributes of the crowd, then and now

Canetti lists four chief attributes (p. 32) of open and closed crowds. Each of these four attributes, he notes, will be found in any crowd to a greater or lesser degree. How do they apply to the electric crowd?

1. "The crowd always wants to grow. There are no natural boundaries to its growth. Where such boundaries have been artificially created – e.g., in all institutions which are used for the preservation of closed crowds – an eruption of the crowd is always possible and will, in fact, happen from time to time."

But the electric crowd has no physical size, because it is discarnate, without tangible or physical aspect; yet it does have infinite mass. Even an electric crowd of two or three members has infinite mass, as does an electric crowd of ten or twenty million members. (Keep this paradox in mind when, for example, imagining the effect on economics: one dollar moving at the speed of light has near-infinite mass and next-to-no size/worth/identity. It may be worthless and can at the same time have the impact of an entire economy based on gold or silver specie. Moving at the speed of light, one dollar can be time-shared by a million or more people at once.) It also has no natural

boundaries: it overleaps all natural and physical limitations, including natural law.

2. "Within the crowd there is equality. This is absolute and indisputable and never questioned by the crowd itself. One might even define a crowd as a state of absolute equality."

For the electric crowd, the "discharge" is absolute and instantaneous; it occurs simultaneously with the shedding of the body, which is to imply that it may be ongoing, a process that is part of the larger, general, electric processing of culture and society.

3. "The crowd loves density. It can never feel too dense...everything must be the crowd itself. The feeling of density is strongest in the moment of discharge."

To the electric crowd, however, proximity and density have no meaning: they make sense only in relation to bodily experience. "Space" is irrelevant as a determinant, although electrically it acquires aesthetic and nostalgic meaning. In its place, the crowd congeals – implodes – via participation, which it uses to establish its being. All electric crowds are invisible: think of the telephone experience, the radio or TV audience, users of the Web or Internet.

4. "The crowd needs a direction... A goal outside the individual members and common to all of them drives underground all the private differing goals which are fatal to the crowd as such. Direction is essential for the continuing existence of the crowd. Its constant fear of disintegration means that it will accept any goal. A crowd exists so long as it has an unattained goal."

Direction, goal, purpose – these are immaterial to the electric crowd. For those who live at electric speed, distant goals make little or no sense; all

futures (and pasts) are here and now. The chiaroscuro of fixed goals relates to the incarnate world of becoming: electricity is absolutist and iconic. All of this goes to reinforce the fact that the electric crowd is unique to our time. Nothing like it has ever before existed in human experience.

The electric crowd is a third kind of crowd, one that has its own properties. It is composed by and of a new type or mode of humankind which, bereft of all traditional ties to the natural world and to natural law, may be something more or less than human.

Three final observations about electric crowds.

1. The biggest need of electric crowds is not to grow, but to BE and to continue to be. In this regard, they resemble closed crowds, which renounce the instability of growth to emphasize permanence. Participational imagery generates the emotion of being, the only reality left after leaving the body and physical existence behind.

2. Participation – the degree of participation – depends on the quality of the imagery. A "good" image is one that allows a lot of participation indepth by a big, that is, diverse, crowd. Our politicians know this profoundly. Superficially, the ego appears to expand to enormous proportions; but like a balloon it is all surface: as it enlarges it becomes more fragile – thinner and emptier. It has to be empty to allow all that participation.

3. The electric crowd's aesthetic, its thrill or emotion, derives from manipulations of being. Each new electric medium conjures a new mode of group being, a new WE. Hybrid energies give the biggest kicks.
It is the nature of electric media to miscegenate and hybridize endlessly.

The mystery is, how could Canetti have made such a profoundly revealing study of crowds and not have noticed that electric media had introduced a new and separate form of crowd, a *tertium non datur*? For the electric crowd is not the result of a synthesis of the open and closed crowds, but a third thing in no way implied in or by either of them, singly or together. For him, as for each of us, that crowd was environmental. As a *ground*, it lets ussee the older kinds of association with great clarity while itself remaining invisible. In order to see any *ground* or environment, some means has to be found to convert it to *figure*. The real significance and use of the arts in Western culture has always been its role of supplying anti-environments.

Canetti revealed a form of association that antedates the crowd: the pack. Each of the several forms of crowd has its etymology in one of the kinds of pack, as the tetrads on the next few pages show. In the pack, the crowd and the crowd crystal are still one. Among the small hordes which roam about as bands of ten or twenty men, he points out, the pack is the universal expression of communal excitement. The very term pack reminds us that the human crowd owes its origin to the example of animals, the pack of animals hunting together.

Characteristic of the pack is the fact that it cannot grow. It is surrounded by emptiness and there are literally no additional people who could join it. It consists of men in a state of excitement whose fiercest wish is to be more. In whatever they undertake together, whether hunting or fighting, they would fare better if there were more of them. (p. 109)

A note on the etymologies of crowds themselves.

The pack forms spontaneously out of the group and most strongly expresses its feeling of unity; it makes up in density for what it lacks in numbers. Of the four essential attributes of the crowd – growth, density, equality, direction – only the last two really exist for the pack; the first two are desired but "only acted." Canetti carefully proposes the pack as an active unit of social organization quite apart from the usual ones dear to anthropologists and sociologists.

I am here deliberately opposing all the usual concepts of tribe, sib, clan, with a different kind of unit, the unit of the pack. Those well-known sociological concepts, important as they are, all stand for something static. The pack, in contrast, is a unit of action, and its manifestations are concrete. To explore the origins of the behaviour

of crowds we have to start from the pack. It is their oldest and most limited form,and it existed long before crowds in the modern sense were known. (pp. 110-111)

The pack has four different forms, or functions. Packs, evidently, all have something fleeting about them, and each changes easily into another.

Just as the natural form of crowd is the open crowd, the natural form of the pack is the hunting pack. It forms whenever the quarry or prey is too strong or fleet or dangerous to be overcome by one man alone.

The second form of pack is the war pack and it has much in common with the hunting pack. It presupposes a second pack against which it is directed. "In earlier times its object was often a single life, one man on whom it had to take revenge. In the certainty with which it knows its victim it comes particularly close to the hunting pack" (p. 111).

The third form is the lamenting pack, which forms whenever a member of a group is lost or dies. Because the group is small, every loss is felt keenly and some kind of action is deemed necessary, whether to protect the group from additional loss or to propitiate the soul of the dead so that it will not turn hostile.

Fourth, Canetti proposes the increase pack to cover the one thing that all packs have in common: the need and the intention to increase.

Increase packs are formed so that the group itself, or the living beings, whether plants or animals, with which it is associated, should become more... Like the other packs they are found everywhere where there are men living together; and what they express is always the group's dissatisfaction with its numbers. (p. 112)

The Open Crowd (the natural crowd)

vortex, density
emphasizes growth;
consumes people

dissolves
direction
discharge (equality)

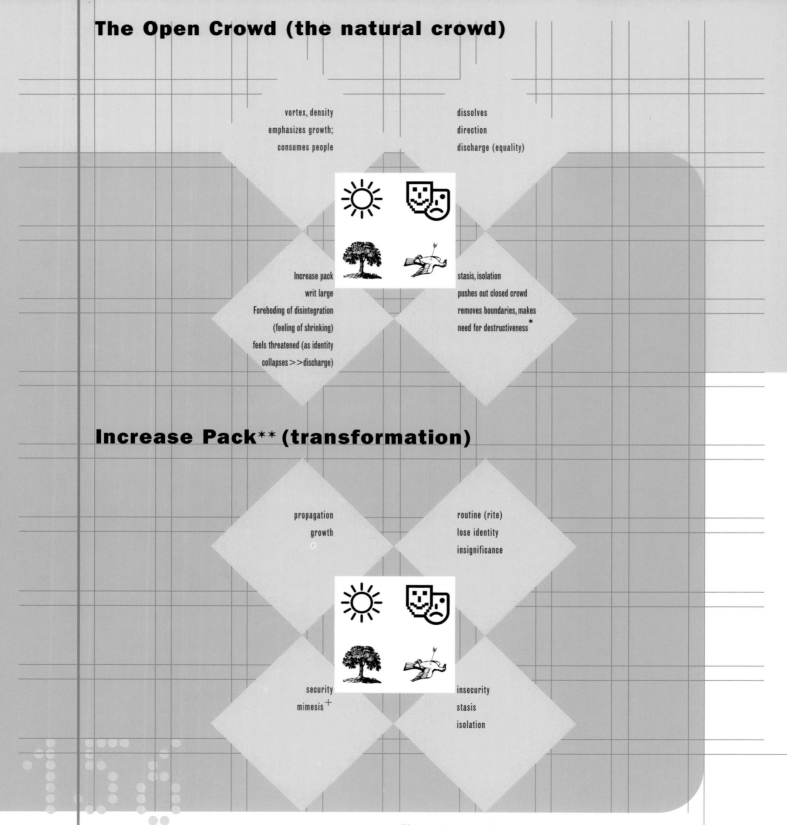

Increase pack
writ large
Foreboding of disintegration
(feeling of shrinking)
feels threatened (as identity
collapses >>discharge)

stasis, isolation
pushes out closed crowd
removes boundaries, makes
need for destructiveness *

Increase Pack** (transformation)

propagation
growth

routine (rite)
lose identity
insignificance

security
mimesis +

insecurity
stasis
isolation

(Notes to these and following tetrads appear on p. 159.)

Closed Crowd (Lamenting Pack)

Emphasizes permanence
(thus creating institutions)#
Rhythmic continuity##
(our next meeting is...)
Emphasis on boundary, order
Limits create density
Stability

Reversal crowd++
(inside flips to out)
Hunting pack≠
Eruption###

Inner

Outer

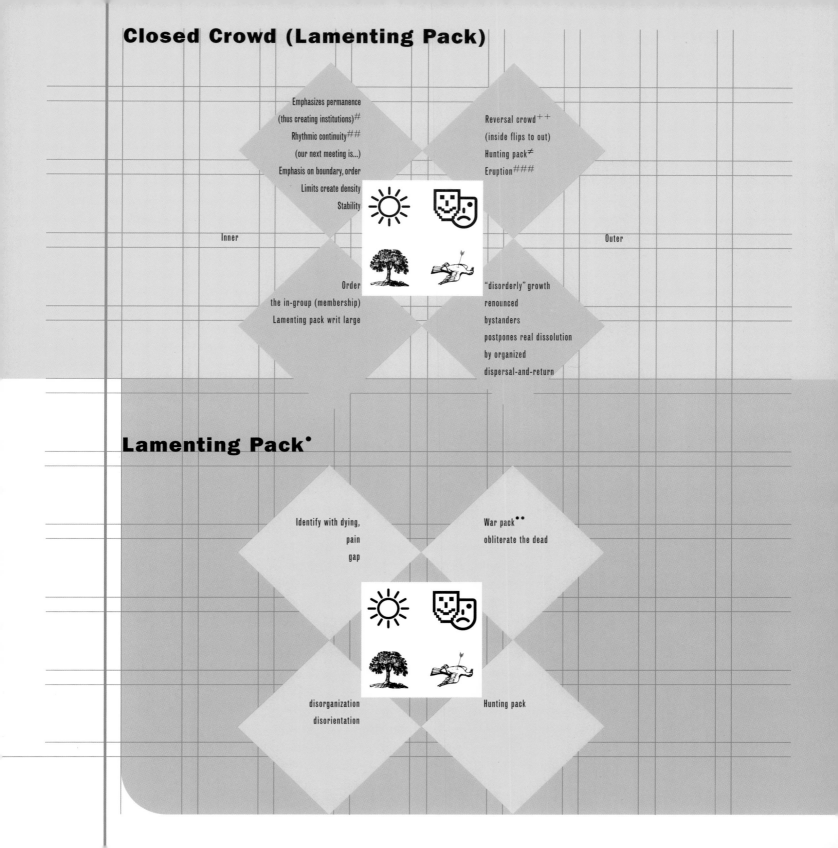

Order
the in-group (membership)
Lamenting pack writ large

"disorderly" growth
renounced
bystanders
postpones real dissolution
by organized
dispersal-and-return

Lamenting Pack•

Identify with dying,
pain
gap

War pack••
obliterate the dead

disorganization
disorientation

Hunting pack

Electric Crowds (discarnate – the dead)

Inner awareness

corporate nature
inner-focussed
Being

the hunter —
of information,
in an information
environment

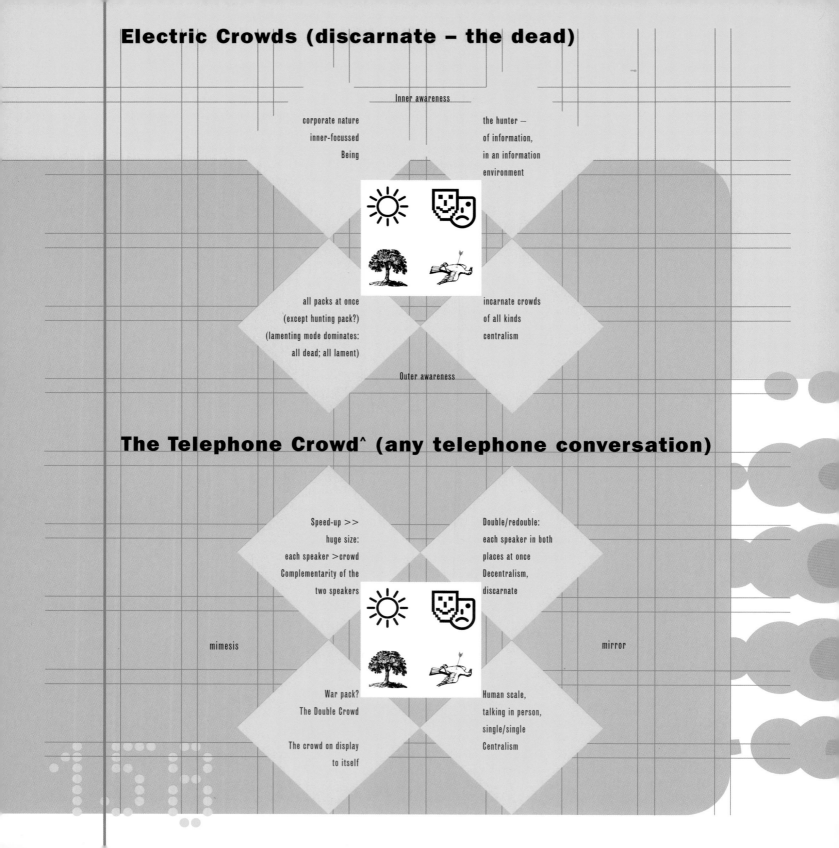

all packs at once
(except hunting pack?)
(lamenting mode dominates:
all dead; all lament)

incarnate crowds
of all kinds
centralism

Outer awareness

The Telephone Crowd^ (any telephone conversation)

Speed-up >>
huge size:
each speaker >crowd
Complementarity of the
two speakers

Double/redouble:
each speaker in both
places at once
Decentralism,
discarnate

mimesis

mirror

War pack?
The Double Crowd

Human scale,
talking in person,
single/single
Centralism

The crowd on display
to itself

Notes to Tetrads

* "In the crowd the individual feels that he is transcending the limits of his own person. He has a sense of relief, for the distances are removed which used to throw him back on himself and shut him in. With the lifting of these burdens of distance he feels free; his freedom is the crossing of these boundaries. He wants what is happening to him to happen to others too; and he expects it to happen to him. An earthen pot irritates him for it is all boundaries. The closed doors of a house irritate him. Rites and ceremonies, anything which preserves, distances, threaten him and seem unbearable" (p. 21).

** "Increase packs are formed so that the group itself, or the living beings, whether plants or animals, with which it is associated, should become more...what they express is always the group's dissatisfaction with its numbers. One of the essential attributes of the modern crowd, namely its urge to grow, thus appears very early, in packs which are not themselves capable of growth" (p. 112).

\+ "In the enormously long period of time during which [man] lived in small groups, he, as it were, incorporated into himself, by transformations, all the animals he knew. It was through the development of transformation that he really became man; it was his specific gift and pleasure. In his early transformations into other animals he acted and danced many of the species which appear in large numbers. The more perfect his representation of such creatures was, the intenser his awareness of their numbers. He felt what it was to be manly and, each time, was made conscious of his own isolation in small groups" (p. 126).

\+\+ A reversal crowd comes into existence for the joint liberation of a large number of people from the stings of command they cannot hope to get rid of alone. They unite to turn on some group of other people whom they see as the originators of all the commands they have borne so long. The important thing is always the dense crowd in the closed room. The boundary prevents disorderly increase, but it also makes it more difficult for the crowd to disperse and so postpones its dissolution.

\# The important thing is always the dense crowd in the closed room. The boundary prevents disorderly increase, but it also makes it more difficult for the crowd to disperse and so postpones its dissolution.

\#\# In the rhythmic crowd (for example the crowd of the dance), density and equality coincide from the beginning. Everything here depends on movement. Density is embodied in the formal recurrence of retreat and approach; equality is manifest in the movements themselves.

≠ Unlike the closed crowd, which emphasizes being and is inwardly-oriented, the pack is a unit of action. All packs have something fleeting about them and they exhibit mutability as a main feature. The first thing which strikes one about the pack is its unswerving direction; equality is expressed in the fact that all are obsessed by the same goal. Here is the reversal of the closed crowd, which is without direction or goal, except to endure. Which kind of pack embodies these characteristics most perfectly? Each pack transforms easily into another. Canetti consistently maintains that the truest and most natural pack is the hunting pack.

\#\#\# In contrast to stability of the closed crowd there is the ebullience or outburst of the open crowd. A crowd quite often seems to overflow from one well-guarded space into the squares and streets of a town where it can move about freely, exposed to everything and attracting everyone. But more important than this external event is the corresponding inner movement: the dissatisfaction with the limitation of the number of participants, the sudden will to attract, the passionate determination to reach all men.

• The Lamenting Pack is so small that it feels every loss as irreplaceable, and unites for the occasion into a pack. The essential thing is the excitement as such, the state of having something to lament in common. The ferocity of the lament, its duration, the amazing rhythm with which it increases and, even after complete exhaustion, starts afresh – all of this proves that what matters here is the reciprocal stimulation to lament. Here are the essential ingredients of the closed crowd.

•• "The inner, or pack, dynamics of war are basically as follows. From the lamenting pack around a dead man there forms a war pack bent on avenging him; and from the war pack, if it is victorious, a triumphant pack of increase....The quick-forming lamenting pack operates as a crowd crystal; it, as it were, opens out, every one who feels the same threat attaching himself to it. Its spirit changes into that of a war pack" (Canetti, p. 162).The inner-directed and self-absorbed flips outward and aggressive.

^ The smallest unit for a telephone conversation is two people, so the Double Crowd is its etymology. By means of electric speed, each person is made legion: an electric Double Crowd in echo-land. Each speaker is both here and there, so the minimum number of participants is really four. There is no crowd crystal for the phone call: each speaker/crowd serves as crystal for the other.

ynesthesia and society

→ **I. The Sensory Foundation for Etymology**

Synesthesia is the term for the way our senses involve each other and transform each other. As an extension of the user, any language is an organ of perception that, like every other medium, enlarges and twists and distorts sensibility. You can say things in French or German, for example, that you cannot even think in English. While formal scientific interest in synesthesia is fairly recent, it provides an unexpected avenue for the study of language as a medium and of media as languages of the senses.

We had the experience but missed the meaning
And approach to the meaning restores the experience
In a different form
– T. S. Eliot, *Four Quartets*, II,
"The Dry Salvages"

Since the Middle Ages, two opposing camps have been arguing over the role of the senses in the medium of language. Nominalists claim that words are mere labels or sign-posts, full stop. Realists – the opposing group – claim that words are more than accidental noises. Instead, for them, words are man-made analogies to things, that is, vocal icons of things. So the word encodes deep in its structure knowledge of the thing named because it is part of the process of knowing. "How," asks the primitive, "would I know Horse if I did not have the word for horse?" The Realist position is behind the entire field of etymology: study of the word traces the process of cognition to knowledge of the thing. This is media study of a high order.

Dr. Richard Cytowic had this to say about the famous synesthete, "S":

S was not aware of any distinct line separating vision from hearing, or hearing from any other sense. He could not suppress the translation of sounds into shape, taste, touch, color, and movement.

Presented with a tone pitched at 2,000 cycles per second, S said, "It looks something like fireworks tinged with pink-red hue. The strip of colour feels rough and unpleasant, and it has an ugly taste – rather like a briny pickle...you could hurt your hand on this."

This same synesthesia enabled him to visualize vividly each word or sound that he heard, whether in his own tongue or in a language unintelligible to himself. The thing to be remembered automatically converted itself without effort on his part into a visual image of such durability that he could remember it years after the initial encounter. So specific was his ability that the same stimuli would produce the exact synthetic response.

S was a person who "saw" everything, who had to feel a telephone number on the tip of his tongue before he could remember it. He could not understand anything unless an impression of it leaked through all his senses. Here is how he described the strange world in which he lived:

"I recognize a word not only by the image it evokes, but by a whole complex of feelings that image arouses. It's hard to express...it's not a matter of vision or hearing but some overall sense I get. Usually I experience a word's taste and weight, and I don't have to make an effort to remember it – the word seems to recall itself. But it's difficult to describe. What I sense is something oily slipping through my hand... or I'm aware of a slight tickling in my left hand caused by a mass of tiny, lightweight points. When this happens, I simply remember, without having to make the attempt."

– R. E. Cytowic, M. D., *The Man Who Tasted Shapes: A Bizarre Medical Mystery Offers Revolutionary Insights into Emotions, Reasoning, and Consciousness* (New York: G. P. Putnam's Sons; A Jeremy P. Tarcher/Putnam Book, 1993), p. 33

Ancient and medieval Grammarians looked at the matter from the other side of the screen, that's all. Realism takes for granted that synesthesia is a normal human response to the things and events that impinge on us. In this view, a word both is a response to an experience, and is itself a form of experience that echoes or is conformal to the stimulus that gave rise to it. Hence, poets have always regarded the language as a store-house of collective experience and energy on which they might draw. T. S. Eliot had this in mind when he wrote, playing on the several meanings of "meaning,"

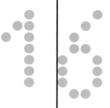

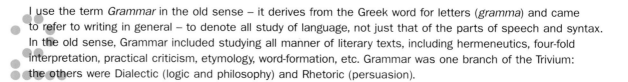

I use the term *Grammar* in the old sense — it derives from the Greek word for letters (*gramma*) and came to refer to writing in general — to denote all study of language, not just that of the parts of speech and syntax. In the old sense, Grammar included studying all manner of literary texts, including hermeneutics, four-fold interpretation, practical criticism, etymology, word-formation, etc. Grammar was one branch of the Trivium: the others were Dialectic (logic and philosophy) and Rhetoric (persuasion).

> We had the experience but missed the meaning,
> And approach to the meaning restores the experience
> In a different form, beyond any meaning
> We can assign to happiness. I have said before
> That the past experience revived in the meaning
> Is not the experience of one life only
> But of many generations – not forgetting
> Something that is probably quite ineffable:
> The backward look behind the assurance
> Of recorded history, the backward half-look
> Over the shoulder, towards the primitive terror.
>   – *Four Quartets*, "The Dry Salvages," II

In these lines, Eliot succinctly rehearses the rationale for etymology as a science that penetrates layer upon layer of meaning of words to reveal the contours of things. Each physical or mental encounter with the world uses the senses in one or another pattern and disturbs their natural equilibrium and harmony. A momentary sequence of such disturbances kicks off the process we call consciousness.

Let the pattern, the disequilibrium, be sustained beyond a moment, and all of the senses reconfigure around

the disturbance, con-forming to it in a new equilibrium, and this process of adjustment we call synesthesia. That pattern,

when expressed vocally by a group, by common consent, adds a word to the language. So a door, encountered by an

Englishman, gives rise to the sound, "door"; by a Roman, "porta"; by a German, "Tür"; by a Russian, "dver"; by a French-

man, "porte," etc. The difference between the various words reflects the differing sensory biases of the languages and

the speakers. Imagine the utterer as an instrument on which things play their music. For a language is not a channel like

telegraph or radio but an organ of collective perception, a way of thinking and seeing and feeling. "S" would appear to

have revealed a new and unexpected kind of "objective correlative" of the word, one registered in human sensation and

experience. A slang consists of a "mutthering pot" of new clichés and old terms recycled for the purpose of updating the

language and bringing it back into sync with the interior synesthesia induced by current experience. When a word passes

out of slang into the wider language, it signals that the group has agreed on the word as a "fit" conscious parallel to its

unconscious synesthesia. What we call the figures or tropes of rhetoric embody certain larger patterns of verbal, mental,

and emotional synesthesia in archetypal form: they are vivisections of the mind and senses in action.

Hence, Grammar's traditional – and usually accounted irrational – emphasis on etymology as producing real

knowledge of things. By digging about among the roots of words, you can discover not only what synesthetic families

(response patterns) a word belongs to, but also you get a snapshot of human perception and experience at various

moments in the history of a culture.

Another and related commonplace in traditional Grammar and poetics is that words store human experience.

This notion prevailed during the oral part of our culture's history and is reasserting itself today. It has perdured among

the poets and writers who attend to and care about language. They have long maintained that the poet's job, as artist,

is in no way related to self-expression in the usual sense, although it is intimately related to expression in the larger

sense. The poet's role is to keep the language in good operating condition, ready to deal with any novelty or present

eventuality. Along the way, if he happens to express himself about something or other, that is neither here nor there,

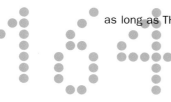

as long as THE JOB is getting done. Again, T. S. Eliot has coasted these shores:

So here I am, in the middle way, having had twenty years –
Twenty years largely wasted, the years of l'entre deux guerres –
Trying to learn to use words, and every attempt
Is a wholly new start, and a different kind of failure
Because one has only learnt to get the better of words
For the thing one no longer has to say, or the way in which
One is no longer disposed to say it. And so each venture
Is a new beginning, a raid on the inarticulate
With shabby equipment always deteriorating
In the general mess of imprecision of feeling,
Undisciplined squads of emotion. And what there is to conquer
By strength and submission, has already been discovered
Once or twice, or several times, by men whom one cannot hope
To emulate – but there is no competition –
There is only the fight to recover what has been lost
And found and lost again and again: and now, under conditions
That seem unpropitious. But perhaps neither gain nor loss.
For us, there is only the trying. The rest is not our business.
– *Four Quartets,* "East Coker," V

If a language is a storehouse of experience, then each language can be regarded as embodying a set of experiences of a particular sort, and each language provides a special shape for the general capacities of people to experience things and to enunciate them. That focus or accent or dialect or idiom or entire language, then, encodes what is unique about the user-group and its particular circumstances and history, namely how their sensory preferences arrange themselves.

In trying to define CIVILIZATION, one poet resorted to synesthesia:

To define it ideogramicly we may start with the "Listening to Incense." This displays a high state of civilization.

In the Imperial Court of Nippon the companions burnt incense, they burnt now one perfume, and now another, or a mixture of perfumes, and the accomplishment was both to recognize what had gone materially into the perfume and to cite apposite poems.

The interest is in the blend of perception and of association.

It is a pastime neither for clods nor for illiterates.

– Ezra Pound, in *Guide to Kulchur* (New York: New Directions, 1970), p. 80

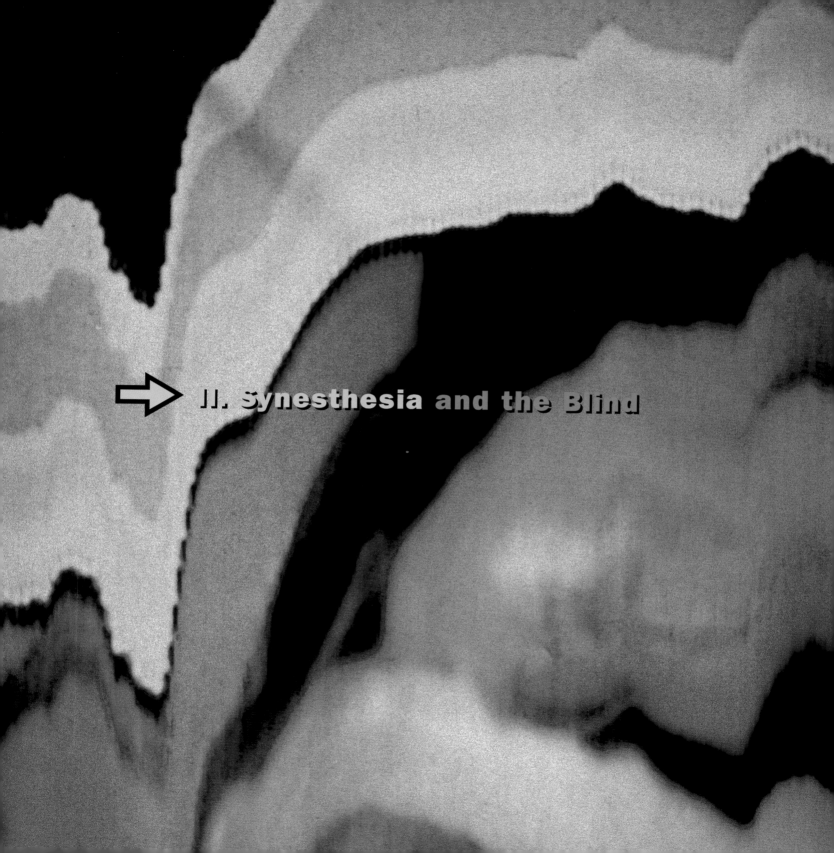

II. Synesthesia and the Blind

Having studied a large number of "sufferers", Dr. Cytowic concluded that synesthesia was not actually exceptional but rather a normal process we all experience unconsciously. His subjects simply were made involuntarily aware of their synesthesia, which he also terms "cross-modal association".

> Cross-modal associations are a normal part of our thinking, although they occur at an unconscious level. In synesthetes...it is as if these associations poke through into awareness, like the sun poking through dark clouds so we can see it and feel its warmth. Even on the cloudiest of days, however, we know that the sun is in the sky even if we can't directly experience it.
>
> Even though we discern what we hear and see as distinct events... experience also shows that we can integrate them in forming thoughts about what these sensations bring to our brains. This integration occurs at a level about which we are unaware. A small number of the human population, called synesthetes, act[s] as if there is a conscious mixing of some of these sensory channels, as if a normal perceptual process that is usually hidden has somehow become bared to their consciousness. – Cytowic, p. 96

For example, one synesthete wrote of the crossover between sound and color and passive touch,

> I most often see sound as colors, with a certain sense of pressure on my skin. I have never met anyone else who saw sound. I'm not sure that "seeing" is the most accurate description. I am seeing, but not with my eyes, if that makes sense. I can't imagine being without my colors. One of the things I love about my husband are the colors of his voice and his laugh. It's a wonderful golden brown, with a flavor of crisp, buttery toast, which sounds very odd, I know, but it is very real. (*Ibid.*, p. 118)

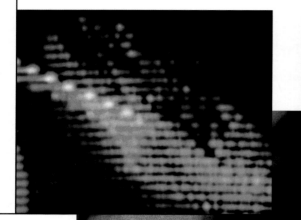
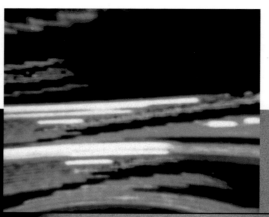

Dr. Cytowic remarks, concerning these observations:

Her comment that "I am seeing, but not with my eyes," was important.
Even when synesthesi are experienced outside of one's body, the
experience is otherworldly. "Seeing" is not done wholly with the eyes
or the mind; perhaps it is best to say that it is done partly with both.
Of course, synesthetes can picture things in their imagination[s] like
anyone else; yet they insist that their synesthetic experiences are
nothing like normal imagination. It is so difficult to describe this
sense of inhabiting two worlds at once, like being half awake yet still
anchored in a dream. (*Ibid.*, pp. 118-19)

And here is a record of a taste-test session with a synesthete:

"It's an organic sphere."

I wrote his description down verbatim next to No. 6, which was

Angostura bitters.

"With tendrils."

I appended Michael's weird elaboration in my notebook. "Organic?"

I prompted.

"The shape feels like a living thing, see, which is why I say 'organic.' It's round but irregular, like a ball of dough."

He cleared his throat. "The quinine, a few flavors back, felt like polished wood because it was so smooth. I guessed that one right away," he smiled. "But this sample is bitter in a different way. It's hard to describe."

He stuck out his tongue. "Gimme another squirt."

I picked up the syringe labeled "6" and squirted a dose onto Michael's tongue.

He shivered and squeezed his eyes together, holding the posture for a few seconds. "Ugh! Where do you get these things?" he choked.

"Tell me what it feels like," I prodded firmly.

"Totally different feel from the quinine," he said, rubbing his fingers together. "It has the springy consistency of a mushroom, almost round," he said as he reached out, "but I feel bumps and can stick my fingers into little holes in the surface."

Michael closed his eyes and swept his hands through the empty air, feeling the shape of the bitter solution I had squirted in his mouth...

"There are leafy tendril-like things coming out of the holes," he said, pulling his hand through the empty air, "about six of them."

"This is a mental image you see?" I asked.

"No, no," he stressed. "I don't see anything. I don't imagine anything. I feel it in my hands as if it were in front of me." (*Ibid.*, pp. 64-65)

At this juncture, it might be useful to refer to the experience of the blind, many of whom experience kindred sensations. Jacques Lusseyran, for example, reports the effect of music in similar terms. As a young boy, he had studied the 'cello for eight years, but found that "music was made for blind people, but some blind people are not made for music. I was among them."

I did not become a musician, and the reason was a strange one. I had no sooner made a sound on the A string, on D or G or C, than I no longer heard it. I looked at it. Tones, chords, melodies, rhythms, each was immediately transformed into pictures, curves, lines, shapes, landscapes, and most of all colors. Whenever I made the A string sound by itself with the bow, such a burst of light appeared before my eyes and lasted so long that often I had to stop playing.

At concerts, for me, the orchestra was like a painter. It flooded me with all the colors of the rainbow.

If the violin came in by itself, I was suddenly filled with gold and fire, and with red so bright I could not remember

having seen it on any object. When it was the oboe's turn, a clear green ran all through me, so cool that I seemed

to feel the breath of night. I visited the land of music. I rested my eyes on every one of its scenes. I loved it till it

caught my breath. But I saw music too much to be able to speak its language. My own language was the language

of shapes.

Strange chemistry, the chemistry which changed a symphony into moral purpose, an adagio into a poem,

a concerto into a walk, attaching words to pictures and pictures to words,, daubing the world with colors and finally

making the human voice into the most beautiful of all instruments! – *And There Was Light*, by Jacques Lusseyran,

Trans. from the French by Elizabeth R. Cameron (Boston: Little, Brown and Company), 1963, pp. 94-95

Before being blinded at eight in a school-yard accident, young Lusseyran was a normal boy (although a bit myopic, so he

wore glasses). Still, he never had experienced any of these "hallucinations" or images before losing his outward sight.

How natural that people who are red should have red shadows. When [Nicole, a friend] came to sit down by

me between two pools of salt water under the warmth of the sun, I saw rosy reflections on the canvas of the

awnings. The sea itself, the blue of the sea, took on a purple tone. I followed her by the red wake which trailed

behind her wherever she went.

Now, if people should say that red is the color of passion, I should answer quite simply that I found that out

when I was only eight years old. (*Ibid.*, p.21)

He goes on, "For my part I had an idea of people, an image, but not the one seen by the world at large."

Frankly, hair, eyes, mouth, the necktie, the rings on fingers mattered very little to me. I no longer even thought

about them. People no longer seemed to possess them. Sometimes in my mind men and women appeared without

heads or fingers. Then again the lady in the armchair rose before me in her bracelet, turned into the bracelet itself.

There were people whose teeth seemed to fill their whole faces, and others so harmonious they seemed to be

made of music. But in reality none of these sights is made to be described. They are so mobile, so much alive that

they defy words.

People were not at all as they were said to be, and never the same for more than two minutes at a stretch.

Some were, of course, but that was a bad sign, a sign that they did not want to understand or be alive, that they were somehow caught in the glue of some indecent passion. That kind of thing I could see in them right away, because, not having their faces before my eyes, I caught them off guard. People are not accustomed to this, for they only dress up for those who are looking at them. (*Ibid.*, p.73)

Moreover, he found that he could read voices like a book. "What voices taught me they taught me almost at once."

I ended by reading so many things into voices without wanting to, without even thinking about it, that voices concerned me more than the words they spoke. Sometimes, for minutes at a time in class, I heard nothing, neither the teacher's questions nor the answers of my comrades. I was too much absorbed by the images that their voices were parading through my head. All the more since these images half the time contradicted, and flagrantly, the appearance of things....

A beautiful voice (and beautiful means a great deal in this context, for it means that the man who has such a voice is beautiful himself) remains so through coughing and stammering. An ugly voice, on the contrary, can become soft, scented, humming, singing like the flute. But to no purpose. It stays ugly just the same....As for hypocrites, they were recognizable immediately. (*Ibid.*, pp. 76-77.)

Lusseyran locates his synesthetic sense of things on a sort of limitless "mental screen."

Names, figures and objects in general did not appear on my screen without shape, nor just in black and white, but in all the colors of the rainbow. Still, I never remember consciously encouraging this phenomenon. Nothing entered my mind without being bathed in a certain amount of light. To be more precise, everything from living creatures to ideas appeared to be carved out of the primordial light. In a few months, my personal world had turned into a painter's studio.

I was not the master of these apparitions. The number five was always black, the letter L light green, and kindly feeling a soft blue. There was nothing I could do about it, and when I tried to change the color of a sign, the sign at once clouded over and then disappeared. A strange power, imagination! It certainly functioned in me but also in spite of me. (*Ibid.*, p. 43)

After a decade of studying this marvelous phenomenon in his own subjects, Dr. Cytowic came to the opinion that synesthesia is a fundamentally mammalian attribute. In other words, he concluded that it is a normal function in every one of us and also that it ordinarily works outside the range of conscious awareness – except in a handful of people. It consists in our ability to translate experience from one form into another, from perception into cognition into recognition, the effect of which we term consciousness. Words do precisely the same: they translate experience from one form (sensory input) into another (vocal). In other words, as translators, every word in every language is a metaphor. Metaphor presents one form of experience in terms of another form: it trans-forms.

A man's reach must exceed his grasp,

Or what's a metaphor?

The synesthete's normal experience is no more hallucination than is the common experience of reading a novel while aware of the chair and the room, and while supplying sights and sounds and smells and characters which are not actually present but are manufactured by the mind to the specifications given by the author. They can be seductively real to the reader, entertaining or terrifying. Crucial, however, is Dr. Cytowic's insistence that synesthesia is utterly normal (and normally suppressed).

I conjectured that synesthesia was a normal brain process, but one that was hidden from the consciousness of all but a handful of the 5.4 billion humans on this planet. I also suggest that the altered states of consciousness I discussed may actually be moments when the "real" us comes to the surface. Things that "we" do not do but which instead "happen" to us, things such as emotions, insights, intuitions, or feelings of certitude, are created by a facet deeper than the one with which we are cognizant.

What we think of as voluntary behavior, set in motion by free will, is really instigated by another part of oursel[ves]. Part(s) of us are inaccessible to self-awareness, the latter being only the tip of the iceberg of who and what we really are. (Cytowic, p. 171)

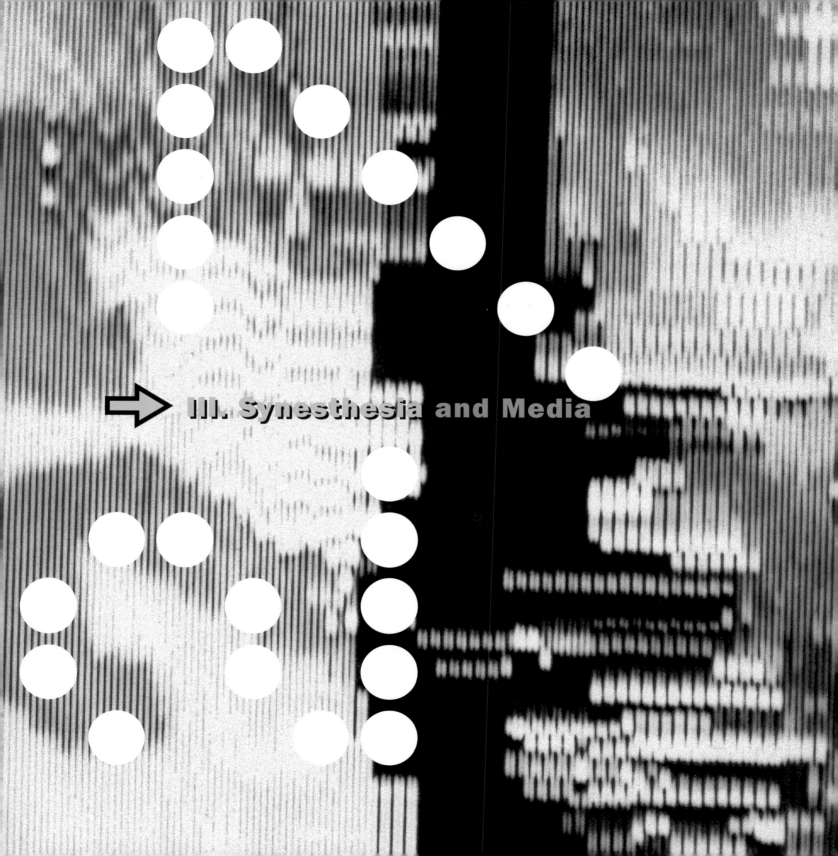

III. Synesthesia and Media

If Dr. Cytowic has the right of it, then synesthesia, as the process of closure, is, together with the conscious stimulus, the very process of knowing itself that has for over a century eluded psychologists. Synesthesia is the body's and the mind's closure-response to any and every experience, to anything that impinges on the senses of the organism. It is what we bring to experience, which is why all experience is 100%. The sensory provocation might induce in response a smell, a taste, a "feel" sensation, a sound, or a combination of these or other sensations or awarenesses. If a fresh experience induces a sound, that is its word, its name; that is how words are born and how they store experience. In this manner are words and etymology together rooted in experience and closure. Another way to put it: words and experience are related as the parts of an analogy. The word is the analogue of the experience or thing it refers to.

Any experience, then, consists of the pair, the input and the closure together, which conform to each other much as the outline of an island and that of the sea that laps its shores conform and change endlessly. Each shapes, conforms to, and con-forms the other. The pattern of sensory input conforms to the stimulus, but the character of response is influenced along certain biases derived from the culture's and the individual's own sensory preferences. Synesthesia does not function in a linear or sequential manner (although it enjoys a special relation to the left hemisphere), but a simultaneous one. Therefore it is not a logical process but analogical, one structured by interval rather than connection. Exactly so are words and metaphor: they, like us, have their being by analogical ratio. So, too, our technologies and ourselves, as the tetrads demonstrate.

The complementary process operates as well. When a child learns a language, he or she learns several things at once besides the meanings of words.

By mimesis, the child learns to put on the patterns of closure for experience established as normal by the culture, to put on all the unconscious group awareness stored in the language, to learn and adopt the labyrinth of experience through miming and imbibing the effects as they have been registered in the music and texture of words. Although we think of speech, the mother tongue, as near and private, there is nothing about us that is so corporate and public. Speech in its subliminal resonance unites us with the most distant ages as well as with the present multitudes. Learning a mother tongue means configuring the labyrinth of cognition and perception – that is, of synesthesia – for life. A language instills the bias that constitutes that particular culture and its particular ways of knowing.

Vestiges of synesthesia make their way into everyday consciousness by the route of sensory illusions and perceptual anomalies. For example, Dr. Cytowic cites the illusion of color constancy:

Color constancy is the illusion in which different stimuli look the same. The problem is that daylight is never the same. Its predominant wavelength, and therefore its color, varies as the sun travels through the sky. Scattering, reflection, and refraction by moisture and dust also change its color from moment to moment. Despite this constant change, a piece of white paper always looks white, an apple red and a banana yellow. People's complexion and clothing also look constant. (Ibid., p. 61)

Either different stimuli can look the same, or the same stimulus can look different, as occurs with a variety of optical illusions such as the classic "Necker cube." Another example is the experience of dyslexics, who see letters of the alphabet skip and tumble on the page in front of their eyes, see letters and words do somersaults and back flips, turn upside-down and inside-out, just like the flip-flop of the Necker cube. So /b/ can masquerade as /p/ or /d/ or /q/; /n/, as /u/; /m/, as /w/, and so on. Entire words will frisk and cavort: "was" becomes "saw" or "sam", and so on. This illusion indicates that one sense is coming into play over the top of another, when for example the eye does the seeing but the hand does the knowing, understanding and interpreting. The hand has no point of view: to the hand only the shape of the letter is all-important, while the orientation is meaningless and irrelevant. Another common illusion, which we literates have all had to learn, but so long ago that we forget ever having found it "unnatural," is the perspective illusion of depth on a plane. We all participate by providing "the beholder's share."

Far less dramatic, because it is so accustomed, is the (again, normal) sensory closure for media – for example, the illusion of motion in movies. The common explanation of seeing motion on the screen is "persistence of vision," but this explanation breaks down in the face of the complementary experience of watching stroboscopic motion. In fact, there is no motion at all in a movie, just a sequence of still images.

All of the motion occurs between the frames, while the screen is in darkness, and is supplied by the viewer. Every sense has a form of space associated with it. Perspective is a construct of visual space – the space brought into play when the eye is abstracted from the other senses. Those intervals on the movie screen are classic examples of kinetic space: the beholder's synesthetic closure is to supply the all of the motion. It is quite impossible to refuse to comply, to decline to supply the motion. These closures are involuntary and unconscious, consequently, for any moviegoer (whether in the theater or the classroom) to claim impartiality or objectivity concerning the events viewed in a film is absurd: he or she has been profoundly involved in constructing every moment of the experience. Nor is it possible to claim detachment

in the face of televised or computerized imagery: the mosaic of dots demands completion by the viewer. Additionally, a computer that boasts a "256-colour spectrum" in its images does not tell the user that it will supply only three of the colors: red, green, and blue. The other 253 are supplied by the viewer from moment to moment, which is one indication of the enormous jump in participation between monochrome and colour screens. Again, the viewer is given no choice in the matter and cannot refuse to comply: the demand of the image is absolute and unrelenting – and terribly addictive. It is not the content of the images that causes the addiction, but the induced sensory closure and the psychic involvement of the limbic system.

By using new techniques for observing blood-flow patterns in the brains of synesthetes, Dr. Cytowic identified the location of synesthesia as the limbic system of the brain, specifically, it resides in "the limbic system of the left hemisphere" (p. 163). He states unambiguously the relation between synesthesia or sensory closure and the part of the brain most intimately involved in language and technological innovation, noting "that synesthesia depends only on the left hemisphere, that a structure called the limbic system is essential for its expression, and most surprising of all, that it does not rely on the brain's cortex" (p. 127). This matter is crucial to media study since the left hemisphere is the fount of utterance of all sorts, embracing not only words but all other kinds of bodily utterance or outering in the forms of technologies.

We are here on the trail of one of the great mysteries of human innovation and society, namely, how are technology and culture intertwined? It was thought that every human technology, as a prosthesis, disturbed the balance of the perceptions and thereby modified the patterns of society. In other words, each major technology meant a new mode of culture and identity, private and corporate. The arts immediately respond with their own synesthesia, to balance or to reveal the new disequilibrium. But we could only guess at the character of those inner processes. There is now no doubt that the cortex and limbic system are reciprocally connected, that each can influence the other. But is either one more influential over the other?

By looking at the direction of flow [of blood] in the brain and the scope of connections with their new methods, authorities in neuroanatomy have clarified that the hippocampus is a point where everything converges. All sensory inputs, external as well as those from our visceral, internal milieu, must pass through the emotional limbic brain before being redistributed to the cortex for analysis, after which they are returned to the limbic system for a

determination whether the highly processed, multisensory information is salient or not. If so, we will likely act; if not, we will ignore it just as we do the majority of the irrelevant energy flux that constantly bombards our nervous system. In determining salience, the emotional brain acts something like a valve, deciding what will grab our attention and what will not.

It turns out that the brain's largest and latest development, the cortex, has more inputs from the limbic system than the limbic system has coming from the cortex. The functional significance of these connections turned out to be the reverse of what we had assumed for decades. Granted there is a reciprocal relation between the cortex and the limbic system, each regulating the other, and each ultimately influencing our mental life. But the number and nature of the recursive feedback circuits ensures that the influence of the limbic system is greater. (*Ibid.*, p. 161)

Furthermore,

One of the reasons that current approaches to artificial intelligence (AI) have failed is that they try to imitate logic and are modeled on the circuitry found in the cortex. They do not take into account that the biologic brain has many different ways of transferring information. To be successful, AI would have to incorporate some kind of regulating system to organize all the different means of information transfer.

In the human brain it is the limbic system that performs this regulation, a fact only recently confirmed in 1985…It turns out that every single division of the nervous system, from the frontal lobes to the spinal cord, contains some component of the limbic system. In other words, the limbic system forms an emotional core of the human nervous system. (*Ibid.*, p. 157)

The limbic system evidently provides equilibration for the individual perceptual body as in their way do the canals of the inner ear for the individual physical body. In a parallel manner, the arts and human cultures serve to provide balance for the social body and the body as extended by technologies.

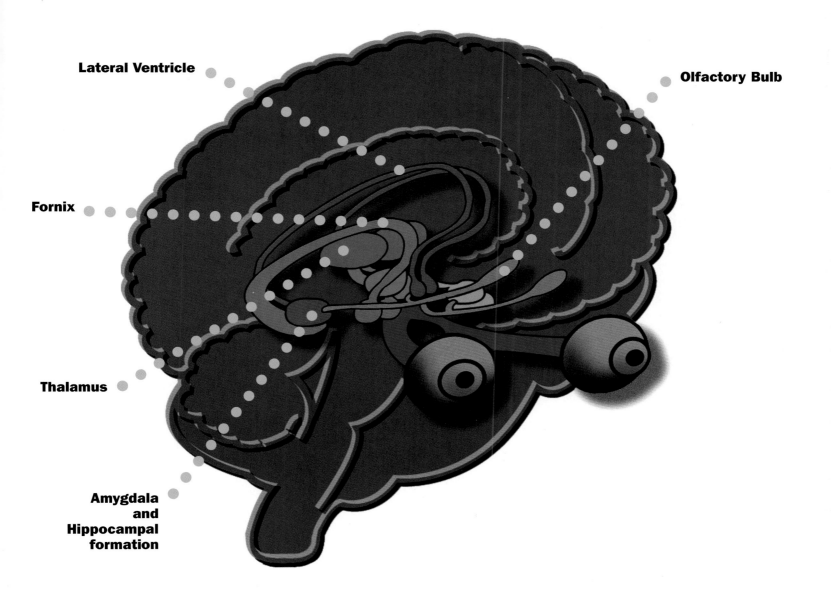

Lateral Ventricle

Olfactory Bulb

Fornix

Thalamus

**Amygdala
and
Hippocampal
formation**

The various parts of the limbic system are linked together; they surround the brainstem like a wishbone. The Fornix

and Hippocampus comprise the swollen bottom tip of each fork: attached to each tip is the Amygdala. The Amygdala,

a mass of nerve cells, is thought to be related to feelings, especially those of rage and aggression. The Hippocampus,

essential in learning, converts information from short- to long-term memory. Egg-shaped Thalamus bulbs are perched

above the brainstem, bond to limbic structures, pass information from the sensory and motor nerves to the brain,

and help regulate consciousness.

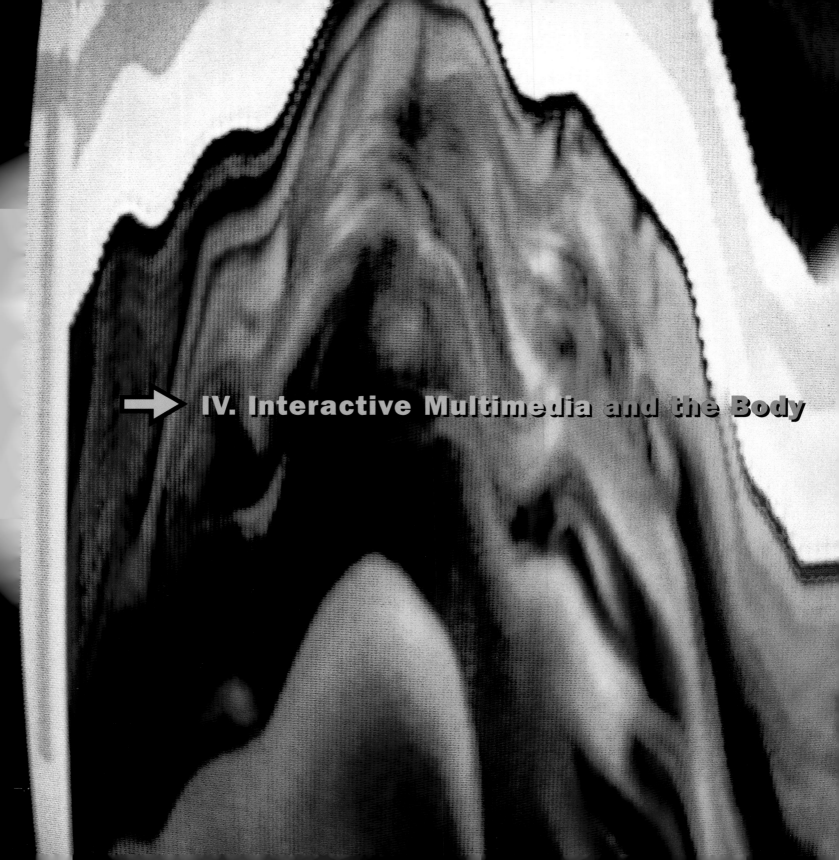

IV. Interactive Multimedia and the Body

Synesthesia is, more and more overtly, being admitted as the grail quest of those involved in developing and exploiting the new field of Interactive Multimedia. Their every attempt is to fill first one and then another sense with information, carefully loading each with packets of stimuli, in order to produce an experience. The approach is additive: adding more and more to one sense, and that to another sense, to another to another. That is to say, by and large, Interactive Multimedia tries to parrot synesthesia, by making it into dramatic entertainment outside the body. But such simple mechanical addition of senses and stimuli remains worlds removed from the real thing. The simple act of loading the sensory apparatus so heavily should be a clue to the condition of the body: it has to be in a pretty numb state to require such a huge input to stimulate it; loading up the stimulus would inevitably result in additional numbing. There is at this stage of development of IM no deftness, no delicacy, no finesse, no subtlety; rather, sheer quantity and brute force. Maslow's Rule may explain why: "the closer a need comes to being satisfied, the larger an increment of additional gratification is required to produce the same satisfaction."

That is, Interactive Multimedia in its current phase provides fake synesthesia – synesthesia for kicks, for amusement and diversion. A new drug. Real synesthesia, natural synesthesia, is always in involuntary play in the healthy organism, below the limb of consciousness, as normal closure for experience. This new forged check is tendered in the form of conscious impact, not by manipulating unconscious closure, and that's the tip-off: making and selling it for sensationalism.

If, as Dr. Cytowic maintains, synesthesia has its base in the limbic system, then IM is humanity's first attempt to extend the limbic system with a technological prosthesis. Our electric media individually and together serve as an external analogy to or prosthesis of the body's central nervous system. When we fling the central nervous system around the world we at once make the physical body obsolete and interiorize all human experience.

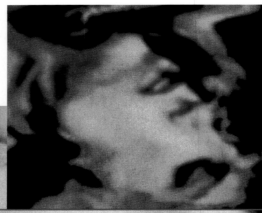

From that moment, the body reverts to the status of a programmable machine made of replaceable spare parts: its new function is to provide aesthetic thrills for the users. This condition was signaled 25 years ago by the birth-control pill and can be seen in our bland acceptance of "designer drugs" (psychedelic, psychotropic, somatic, and psychosomatic) today. Drugs as much as Virtual Reality – the newest fad – parody this condition of interiorization of all experience. VR cuts off the user from all outer experience as irrelevant and intrusive and shifts the play to the interior landscape instead. Making all experience interior experience means that the roles of the limbic system and the inner ear have been effectively reversed. Perhaps fortunately, all that Interactive Multimedia can manage at present is not so much real analogy as parody of real synesthesia. But what might be the consequences, should the attempt succeed?

Every technology, that is, every extension, externalizes some faculty or organ of the body. Each new one establishes a new analogical ratio among the parts of the body that puts on the new extension or prosthesis.

Any invention or technology is an extension or self-amputation of our physical bodies that demands new ratios or new equilibriums among the other organs and extensions of the body. There is, for example, no way of refusing to comply with the new sense ratios or sense "closure" evoked by the TV image. But the effect of the entry of the TV image will vary from culture to culture in accordance with the existing sense ratios in each culture…To behold, use or perceive any extension of ourselves in technological form is necessarily to embrace it. To listen to radio or to read the printed page is to accept these extensions of ourselves into our personal system and to undergo the "closure" or displacement of perception that follows automatically. It is this continuous embrace of our own technology in daily use that puts us in the Narcissus role of subliminal awareness and numbness to them as servomechanisms. That is why we must, to use them at all, serve these objects, these extensions of ourselves, as gods or minor religions. An Indian is the servomechanism of his canoe, as the cowboy of his horse…

– Marshall McLuhan, *Understanding Media* (New York: New American Library, 1964, Rpt., M.I.T. Press, 1965), pp.45-46

…or the typist of his word-processor. Narcissus had no awareness whatever that he was entranced by his own amputated image. He would have been horrified to learn the truth. No more is the user of media aware of his addiction to his own self-amputation or closure. The fate of Narcissus's girlfriend, Echo, dramatizes deeper dimensions of the myth. Narcissus, paralyzed by his own image, simply ignored Echo – representing sensory balance and synesthesia – and she slowly wasted away.

Any new extension represents a sudden outward amplification of some faculty or organ, a hyperaesthesia that induces an inward anesthesia. We may expect that externalizing our synesthesia will have the most profound effect on the psyches of those so extended in numbing – what, exactly? their ongoing natural synesthesia?

The principle of numbness comes into play with electric technology, as with any other. We have to numb our central nervous system when it is extended and exposed, or we will die. Thus the age of anxiety and of electric media is also the age of the unconscious and of apathy. But it is strikingly the age of the consciousness of the unconscious, in addition. With our central nervous system strategically numbed, the tasks of conscious awareness and order are transferred to the physical life of man, so that for the first time he has become aware of technology as an extension of his physical body. Apparently this could not have happened before the electric age gave us the means of instant, total field-awareness. With such awareness, the subliminal life, private and social, has been hoicked up into full view, with the result that we have "social consciousness" presented to us as a cause of guilt feelings. Existentialism offers a philosophy of structures, rather than categories, and of social involvement instead of the bourgeois spirit of individual separateness or points of view. In the electric age we wear all mankind as our skin. (*Ibid*, p. 47)

Every act of knowing is also an act of ignoring. Perhaps this new technology conceals a psychic peril of a kind we have not confronted before. Never before have we been able to make of synesthesia itself a commercial artifact.

The serious artist follows the natural lines of force and does it by limning and miming the perceptual labyrinth of closure. Given this new technology, the artist's job now moves to orchestrating the senses, to overtly organizing sensory closure and using multimedia and all manner of convergence appropriate to the job. "The job" understood to mean not just that of restoring health and balance: to do so is to use art in its therapeutic capacity (a perfectly legitimate use). But art has twin capacities, each therapeutic in its way. The one, counterbalance of present excess; the other, inoculation against present addiction and susceptibility. This latter move generally occurs by means of satire; it restores sensibility to numbed areas and insulates them against further numbing by environmental forces.

Art is a response to a cultural situation that has reached a certain intensity. Wyndham Lewis used to point out that the artist is engaged in writing a detailed history of the future because he is the only one who can see the present. That is to notice that most people are always adjusting to past situations and robotizing themselves in an effort to conserve stability. But artists, because they spend their energies training their sensibilities, have learned how to tune in to present situations that are completely beyond the perceptual grasp of the ordinary person. So serious art is always some fifty or more years ahead of technology in structuring awareness of coming patterns and activity.

The great poet should not only perceive and distinguish more clearly than others the colors or sounds within the range of ordinary vision and hearing; he should perceive vibrations beyond the range of ordinary people and be able to make others see and hear more at each end of the spectrum than they could ever see without his help.

It is therefore a constant reminder to the poet of the obligation to explore, to find words for the inarticulate, to capture those feelings which people can hardly even feel, because they have no words for them; and at the same time a reminder that the explorer beyond the frontier of ordinary consciousness will only be able to return and report to his fellow-citizens if he has all the time a firm grasp upon the realities with which they are already acquainted… The task of the poet, in making people comprehend the incomprehensible, demands immense resources of language; and in developing the language, enriching the meaning of words and showing how much words can do, he is making possible a much greater range of emotion and perception for other men, because he gives them the speech in which more can be expressed. – T. S. Eliot, "What Dante Means to Me" in *To Criticize the Critic and Other Writings* (New York: Farrar, Straus & Giroux, 1965), p. 134

In other words, in expressing what other people feel, the poet, the artist, is also changing the feeling by making it more conscious; he is making people more aware of what they feel already and thereby teaching them something about themselves. He can make his readers share consciously in new feelings and sensibilities which they had not consciously experienced before. This is the difference, explains Eliot, between the writer who is merely eccentric or mad and the genuine or serious artist. The mad writer may have feelings which are unique but which cannot be shared, and are therefore useless. The genuine artist discovers in the present environment new variations of sensibility which can be appreciated by others. Our sensibility is constantly changing as the world about us changes: in giving expression to new awareness, the serious artist is developing and enriching the language in which he works. Art, thus, is always prophetic because the artist has holistic awareness in contrast to the fragmentary awareness of the merely practical man.

Interactive multimedia, while serving to provide synesthesia for the disembodied, holds the promise of a new convergence of the arts. Every new technology brings with it new intensity of awareness and new impercipience. Each new technology means, therefore, a new mode of culture and also a new mode of art. But it is in the nature of electric technologies, unlike the mechanical forms of the preceding ages, to hybridize incessantly and generate ever new extensions and extrapolations of themselves. The current expression for this tendency to produce unexpected hybrids is "technological convergence" but that term blinds us to the concomitant cultural convergings occurring in the *ground*. Operating at the speed of light, electric technologies work in a world of simultaneous relations and possibilities: they naturally combine and intermarry unceasingly. Hardware technologies, far slower, operate sequentially, one-thing-at-a-time, and move instead in the direction of specialized form and function.

IM bespeaks new hybrids of culture and arts and present us with the pattern of future innovation as equally hybrid. We live on the threshold of rediscovering the common language of the arts and sciences, a language lost during the centuries of specialism just past. It is no longer enough to practice just one art: the artist of our time must become amphibian and polylingual, able to command expression in several arts simultaneously.

Formerly, new technologies appeared once a generation or two, and we had time to accommodate ourselves and our cultures to conform to their demands. Presently, innovations of incredible transforming power appear not every generation but every three or four years, leaving ordinary mortals inadequate time to adjust to the new circumstances. All of the new technologies exercise their power and influence globally: all cultures are now global cultures. All arts, then, also have to go global. The merely regional artist, the single-culture specialist artist is irrelevant to today's needs.

The pressure to retreat to the robotic condition of the well-adjusted, has never been stronger.

The arts have been transforming, these last few years, into handicrafts and into more general pursuits or fancies. Today, no sharp distinction shows between serious art and amateur dalliance, whereas a generation ago such distinctions were commonplace. Synesthesia by the arts, then, appears to be spreading into the culture at large as art becomes everybody's province rather than the preoccupation of a few specialists.

Meanwhile, the arts as a navigational aid have grown indispensable to cultural and psychic survival in the electric information age.